FAITH WITHOUT FEAR

"There are many books on evangelism, but what sets *Faith Without Fear* apart from so many others is its brevity, practicality, and inspiration. You will be excited and equipped to share your faith in a shockingly short amount of time. The appendix on creating a culture of evangelism is worth the price of the book alone. What a great resource for individuals, small groups and entire churches who want to take more seriously the call to fulfill the Great Commission."

GARY THOMAS
Best-selling author of *Sacred Romance*

"If you've ever wondered how to fulfill the Great Commission by starting in your own back yard, with the people you know and new ones you meet, look no further. *Faith Without Fear* is an outstanding and practical guide on how to start the faith conversation, and challenge new thinking and growth in those around us. Very worthwhile read.

STEPHEN ARTERBURN
Founder, New Life Ministries and Host of *New Life Live*

"Jeff has a naturally magical way of communicating to people. He reaches down into a person's heart and is able to draw out that person's inner-most being. It is always a joy to speak with him. In *Faith Without Fear*, Jeff Jerina, shares his greatest talent and applies his secrets of communication to one of most Christians' greatest struggles: Sharing our faith. Communicating to others what God has done for us ideally ought to be one of the most natural things we do as children of God, yet most believers I know (including myself) struggle with sharing the good news that Jesus is the Messiah who can save us! I appreciate Jeff greatly because he is a well-trained, seminary graduate theologian who has never lost his ability to communicate with the average person. He is down to earth in his everyday conversation. I have watched him as he interacts with people he doesn't know. He loves and values everyone the same. I believe if the church could grasp his ability to communicate the gospel, we could convert billions of people across the world to become disciples of Jesus Christ in a very short time."

DR. STEVEN L. SMITH
President, Digging Deep
Author of *The Early Church on Fire: Re-igniting the Passion of the First Followers of Jesus*

"In *Faith Without Fear*, Jeff Jerina inspires and equips born-again believers to fulfill the Great Commission. As your evangelism coach, Jeff provides a step-by-step guide for sharing the hope of Jesus Christ with others. This book will give you the confidence to share the gospel with anyone you come in contact with."

JC WATTS, JR.
Former Oklahoma Congressman

"Jeff has answered the nagging question of so many Christians. How do I start a conversation about Jesus with a non-believer? Read *Faith Without Fear* and apply it and watch God transform the world through you. When you get to heaven one day, the only thing that will matter is, will there be anyone there because I allowed Jesus to speak through me. The information in this book will help us say a resounding "YES!"

DAVID L. COOK
Author and Executive Producer: *Seven Days in Utopia*

"Jeff Jerina's inspirational book, *Faith Without Fear*, will inspire you with his testimony, equip you in a relevant and practical way, and challenge you to live an intentional life as Christ commanded. Enjoy the journey!"

STEVE FEDYSKI
COO, Pure Flix Entertainment

"The Bible says the 'gospel' is of foremost importance (1 Cor. 15) Knowing this good news and sharing it with others is central to the calling of every man of God. Through his national talk show, Jeff Jerina has emerged a uniquely qualified and passionate voice to men about what it means to be a "gospel-ed" man who doesn't chicken out when the souls of men are on the line. Now in his new book *Faith Without Fear*, Jeff will help equip you in practical ways to talk to others about God's gospel and the new life He offers in Christ Jesus. Wherever God has planted you, let Jeff coach you up to spread the good infection of the life transforming gospel."

DAVE BROWN
Pastor and Director
Washington Area Coalition of Men's Ministries (WACMM)

"It has been my privilege to have Jeff Jerina as a graduate student at Liberty Theological Seminary. An excellent student who is passionate about worship of our Lord, Jeff has learned that the greatest act of worship is obedience. That, in turn, has become a motivating force in his life. Obedience to the call of Christ to "take the gospel to the ends of the earth," and to then "make disciples." Jeff incorporates his passion for evangelism with his God-given creativity. In *Faith Without Fear*, you will discover the scriptural mandate for sharing the gospel in a new, refreshing, and creative way."

DR. RODNEY D. WHALEY
Assistant Professor of Music and Worship
Liberty University School of Music

"Many are indicating a great harvest of souls is before us. We need evangelists to rise up and share the gospel. *Faith Without Fear* is a training and equipping manual to encourage every seasoned and new believer to reach out to their God-given sphere of influence. May God stir us to win souls for Christ."

RICK WARZYWAK
Transformation Michigan/MI Oak Initiative

"Driven by a passion to tell the world just how good his Savior is, Jeff doesn't witness to lost people about Christ because he feels indebted, but because he feels overwhelmed at what the Savior and salvation did for him. Thus, the book you are about to explore is not only backed by his many experiences in reaching the lost for whom Christ died, it is written in such a way that believers who are as grateful as Jeff can learn to reach folks around them the same way he does. Enjoy!"

BRAD STRAND
Author of *Strand Study Bible*

"Have you ever wondered how you will handle the "witness opportunity" when it presents itself? I sure have. In *Faith Without Fear*, Jeff Jerina provides the tools and knowledge to feel confident when the wonderfully inevitable happens! Thank you, Jeff!"

DAVID FUESS
CEO, Catapult Systems
Best-selling author of *Why They Buy*

"Many of us remember the moment we trusted Jesus Christ as our Lord and Savior. We can see how God has miraculously transformed our lives that we naturally want others to experience that same freedom. However, when presented with an opportunity to share the gospel, we may not know what to say. You may even feel like you're not qualified to do so. In *Faith Without Fear*, Jeff Jerina shows you how to confidently and accurately share the good news. So regardless of your background, vocation, or biblical knowledge this must-read book will encourage and equip you in sharing your faith to anyone you come across."

DR. JAMIE ATEN
Founder and Executive Director
Humanitarian Disaster Institute, Wheaton College

"I've heard it said that there are only two kinds of people who don't like "evangelism", Christians and non-Christians. Jeff's book, *Faith Without Fear*, not only reminds us that building the kingdom is an essential part of being a follower of Jesus, he also gives us practical advice on how to overcome the fear of doing so. Let's do this!"

JOHN GROOTERS
President, Grooters Productions

FAITH

—— *without* ——

FEAR

How to Share What You Believe
with Confidence and Power

JEFF JERINA

For other books, training, and resources
visit JeffJerina.com

For more information or to schedule an interview, contact:
Jeff@MenUnplugged.net
www.JeffJerina.com

ISBN 978-1-7341419-5-5 (paperback)
ISBN 978-1-7341419-0-0 (ebook)

Sales of this book support Jeff Jerina in reaching others for Jesus Christ, equipping Christians to share their faith, and providing biblical solutions to help men and their families succeed in life.

Learn more at www.JeffJerina.com

Published by: Olive Tree Publications, Wylie, TX
Printed in the United States of America

For discounts on books, live or virtual training with Jeff Jerina, and other online training courses by Jeff, please visit **www.JeffJerina.com.**

DEDICATION

To my wife, Amy—thank you for loving me and joining me in this incredible journey we call life. Your encouragement and unwavering support have helped me cross the finish line in so many endeavors, including this book.

To my children, Kinley and Eli—you are an amazing blessing and gift from God. Thank you for bringing me joy and laughter. I am so proud of who you are.

To my mom and dad—thank you for always being there for me. For teaching me the value of hard work and perseverance, and for modeling God's love and forgiveness.

CONTENTS

CONTENTS

FOREWORD

BY JOSH MCDOWELL

T he best decision I ever made was when I trusted Jesus Christ as my Lord and Savior. That one decision changed the course of my life for good (not just now, but for all eternity). Since then, it has been my mission to tell people that God loves them, that He wants a personal relationship with them, and to equip the Church to do the same.

As more people seek real answers to the problems they face, an unconditional love, and a hope that never ends, the time for Christians to share the gospel is now! For we know the ultimate solution—a personal and everlasting relationship with Jesus Christ.

Jeff and I spoke for the first time in 2018 on his talk show, Men Unplugged. I immediately noticed his passion for reaching the lost and equipping fellow believers to do the same. I was impressed by his interview style and focus on helping others ignite their faith in Christ.

When he told me about *Faith Without Fear*, I was excited to be a part of it. I found it refreshing to read an evangelism book that encourages and equips Christians to fulfill the Great Commission.

Like a great coach, this book will give you the training and inspiration to proclaim the life-saving message of Jesus Christ with confidence and skill.

Faith Without Fear, by author Jeff Jerina, provides a simple yet proven method for sharing the gospel to anyone you come across.

His personal testimony is proof of how God's grace and a faithful believer in sharing it, can reach anyone through the work of Jesus Christ. Jeff's inspirational stories, biblical truths that he shares, step-by-step training, and interactive questions are tools that anyone can use to proclaim the good news.

Readers will be amazed at how quickly they will learn how to share their faith, overcome obstacles, and be proactive when it comes to reaching the lost. Seasoned evangelists will get an extra boost of motivation to continue the good fight.

Regardless of whether or not you work in full-time ministry or have the gift of evangelism, you will learn how to simply and accurately share the gospel. Your fears about witnessing will subside as you progress through each easy-to-follow lesson.

Imagine the benefits of knowing that no matter where you are or whom you're speaking with, you will always be ready to share your faith, without fear or hesitation. Your ability to start a spiritual conversation will improve as you understand the Holy Spirit is right there with you every step of the way. Your walk with the Lord will strengthen as you learn what your role and God's role is in sharing the gospel.

Right away, you'll get the necessary tools and relevant Scripture to accurately tell others about the good news of Jesus Christ. You will be encouraged as you learn that anyone (regardless of age, vocation, or experience) can learn how to share the gospel. As you will learn in this book, all it takes is practice.

Ultimately, this work will help you bring glory to God as we expand His kingdom together.

So, get ready to dive into a book that will unlock your witnessing skills! One that will prepare you for the greatest mission on earth—fulfilling the Great Commission.

Josh McDowell

Josh McDowell Ministries in Plano, Texas

PREFACE

The content of this book is taken from an evangelism course I developed in 2008. It's the culmination of God's radical work in my life and the passion He's given me to share the gospel.

Since placing my faith in Jesus Christ in August 2001, I've been compelled to tell others about God's free gift of salvation. As excited as I was to share my testimony back then, I routinely stopped short of telling others about the good news itself. Why?

Quite simply, I never learned *how* to witness.

Thankfully, that all changed in the summer of 2005 after I received some informal evangelism training. That coaching gave me the confidence and knowledge to accurately proclaim the good news of Jesus Christ.

I also realized: If God can use a redeemed prodigal like me, He can use anyone—including YOU!

Three years later, a church in Dallas, Texas asked me to train individuals and mission teams on evangelism. You can imagine my excitement. Especially since I was so eager to share all the Lord had shown me.

I didn't wait. I accepted the invitation with joy and enthusiasm. After spending hours compiling everything I learned, supporting the material with Scripture, and creating a course layout that would work for individuals and groups I was ready to teach.

By the grace of God, the class was a big success. The impact it made on each participant motivated me to tell others about the hope of Christ even more. In addition, their newly acquired confidence, understanding, and ability to share the gospel revealed something new about my own ministry. It taught me that my job as an evangelist is more than just seeking and setting captives free; it includes helping others do the same (see Eph. 4:11-12).

Armed with a new desire to see Christians share their faith, I began asking fellow believers about their personal experiences with witnessing. Their responses troubled me, as most of them stated:

- They had rarely or never shared the gospel.
- They lacked the confidence or competence to do so.
- They were afraid to share their faith with someone else.
- They didn't want to offend anyone.
- They really didn't think much about it.

I realized that I had been where they were—with a hunger to share the gospel—but for these same reasons I never did. Thus, I felt I needed to do something about it—something that would help believers share their *Faith Without Fear*.

So, I began searching for a way to bridge the gap between a believer's lack of experience in presenting the gospel and his or her genuine desire to reach the lost. What I discovered was that almost every reason that evangelicals have for not sharing their faith stems from one thing: *They've never been taught how to witness.*

But here's the great news! You and every other Christian (regardless of biblical knowledge, vocation, or spiritual gifts) can learn how to share the gospel. All it takes is *practice.* That's where this book comes in.

As your evangelism coach, this book will give you the training and relevant Scripture to accurately tell others about the good news of Jesus Christ. It will motivate and inspire you to respond to those divine witnessing opportunities with confidence and zeal.

Thus, it's my hope and prayer that this work will: Equip you in becoming a more passionate and proficient soul-winner, remove any fears that you may have about witnessing, and remind you that your personal story of salvation matters.

So, buckle up.

Get ready.

And prepare to set the captives free.

INTRODUCTION

If God's love for mankind is such that no one shall perish (and it is) and God gave all believers the authority and directive to proclaim the good news (and He has), then why aren't more Christians doing their part in reaching the lost?[1] In my opinion, it's because many believers have never learned *how* to share the hope of Christ with others.

Consequently, numerous Christians are fearful when it comes to sharing their faith. Others worry that they'll be rejected or persecuted for the cause of Christ. Some think the job of evangelism is reserved for individuals in full-time ministry. Perhaps you've thought or said something like this, I don't witness because:

- I'm afraid of telling the person something wrong.
- I don't want to confuse the individual I'm speaking with.
- I don't want to offend anyone.
- I don't know how to start a spiritual conversation.
- I don't want my friends to feel like I'm judging them.
- I don't know how to put it all together.
- What if they ask me something I don't know the answer to?

As I sit in my study writing this introduction, I remember having these same thoughts. However, as I learned how to share the gospel, an amazing thing happened—my fears went away. The same thing can happen to you. You can overcome any fear or anxiety you have about sharing your faith as you learn and apply the lessons outlined in this book.

WHAT'S IN IT FOR YOU

Chances are you've heard the expression, *practice makes perfect*, which is true! Whether it's learning to walk, brushing your teeth, riding a bike, or something as intricate as performing brain surgery; you have to learn *how* to do those things before you can actually do them well. Let alone, ensuring that you execute them without hesitation or fear. The same is true for anyone who wants to tell others about the life-saving message of Jesus Christ. You have to learn *how* to witness first. All it takes is some basic training.

That my friend, is the purpose of this book—to be your guide. Walking you through step-by-step on how to accurately share the good news of Jesus Christ to anyone you come across. Leaving no stone unturned, you'll be encouraged and equipped as this course contains:

- easy to follow lessons
- real-life witnessing stories
- a simple template for personal evangelism
- biblical explanations
- practical examples to unleash your witnessing skills

In the same token, I truly believe that you'll discover something the Lord taught me years ago: It's not the 'capacity' to learn, but the 'willingness' to prepare that really matters!

Did you get that? Your ability to present God's plan of salvation has nothing to do with your education, vocation, or biblical knowledge. On the contrary, it has everything to do with your *desire* to prepare. If you're wondering whether or not God wants to use you in this—His ultimate rescue ministry, the answer is an emphatic "Yes!" If you don't believe me, check this out.

> IT'S NOT THE 'CAPACITY' TO LEARN, BUT THE 'WILLINGNESS' TO PREPARE THAT REALLY MATTERS.

WHERE YOU FIT IN

God has given the Great Commission to each and every believer, regardless of whether or not you have the gift of evangelism. As a matter of fact, Scripture excludes no one from Christ's directive (see Acts 1:8; Mt. 28-16-20; Mark 16:15; John 20:21; 2 Cor. 5:18-21). F. B. Meyers wrote:

> Your personal witness for Christ is an imperative obligation. You cannot evade it by any excuse as to your temperament, your nervousness, or your circumstances. The King makes no exceptions. His command is decisive. If we belong to His Church, we are bound to proclaim His love and death to every creature within our reach.[2]

K.P. Yohannan notes, "Evangelism is not just for full-time workers, but for every child of God."[3] Yohannan goes on to say that "Our one purpose is this: To somehow, some way, win the lost at all costs and prepare them for the coming of the Lord."[4]

By the same token, Robert Coleman holds that: "Evangelism is not an optional accessory to [a Christian's] life. It is the heartbeat of all that we are called to be and do."[5]

So, my question to you is this: Will you take Christ's marching orders seriously?

Awesome! Because you answered "Yes" to the question above, you're about to embark on the greatest journey of all—setting the captives free. As your brother in Christ, I look forward to joining you on this noble quest.

> YOUR ABILITY TO PRESENT GOD'S PLAN OF SALVATION HAS NOTHING TO DO WITH YOUR EDUCATION, VOCATION, OR BIBLICAL KNOWLEDGE.

FOR MORE HELP

If you need additional training, I also offer an evangelism course that you can take online or in a group setting. Combined together, your witnessing skills will be sharpened even more. You can also hear well-known and inspiring Christian leaders share their personal testimonies on my interview-based talk show, *Men Unplugged*. For more information about the course, my group training, or the *Men Unplugged podcast* please visit my personal website at **JeffJerina.com**.

CHAPTER 1

PROOF IN THE NUMBERS

The harvest truly is plentiful, but the laborers are few.
Matthew 9:37

Research performed by Win Arn and Gary McIntosh illustrates the eternal impact that believers have within their own circles of influence. Arn's survey (of over 17,000 Christians) revealed that 90 percent of born-again believers came to faith through either a friend or a relative.[1] The remaining 10 percent made a faith-based decision as a direct result of a pastor's witnessing efforts or church experience.

More recently, McIntosh published a similar study in 2014. His findings disclosed that family members, friends, lay leaders, neighbors, and co-workers were responsible for 83 percent of new decisions for Christ, whereas full-time ministers accounted for just 17 percent of those commitments.[2]

Wow! That's incredible.

Seriously, these reports reveal some interesting data. They conclude that the overwhelming majority of individuals who commit their life to Jesus, do so through the direct involvement of a friend or a family member. Even from a conservative perspective, the numbers say it best. They tell us that 8 out of every 10 born-again believers change their eternal destination through the influence of someone other than a clergyman.

A WIN-WIN-WIN SITUATION

Hopefully, these surveys will help you see the importance that you have in reaching the lost. As a result, I pray you're encouraged to step out in faith and share the good news with others. When you do, you can be confident in knowing that as you plant the seeds of the gospel—you cannot fail—regardless of the outcome. Even if those individuals reject Christ as their Lord and Savior. Why? Because your success in evangelism is not based on the end result. It's based on your faithfulness to proclaim His name.

In other words, you can't lose. Every time you share the good news, you're in a *win-win-win* situation. It's a *win* because you were faithful in sharing your faith. It's another *win* because the gospel was heard by another human being. It's the ultimate *win,* the moment a non-believer accepts God's free gift of salvation.

THE KEY WORD IS...

As true as these statements are, Dr. Bill Bright (founder of Campus Crusade for Christ) stated that, "Only 2 percent of today's church is actively involved in evangelism."[3] Now, if Bright is correct, then 98 percent of believers are disengaged in the ministry of evangelism. That's 2.25 billion out of 2.3 billion Christians as of 2017.[4] Don't you think we can do better than that? I do!

Okay, you may be thinking, *Wait a second, Jeff. Two percent sounds really low.* I agree! However, the key word here is the word 'actively'. It implies someone who consistently looks for opportunities to share their faith. In other words, that Christian is proactive about initiating and engaging in conversations with the intent and action of verbally sharing the gospel with others. With this in mind, I hope you can understand why Bright's comment is so relevant to the state of evangelism in the Church today.

THE GOSPEL WOULD SPREAD

Consider the following scenario: Imagine if every Christian shared the gospel to a different person each year. If so, the entire world's population would have a chance to hear about Christ's atoning sacrifice in less than two and a half years.[5] Hands down, it would be the greatest evangelistic endeavor anyone has ever seen. In that short amount of time:

- The gospel would spread like wildfire.
- Hearts would transform.
- Christians across the globe would be on fire for Jesus.

Trust me. I know this is a radical concept. But isn't that what Christianity is all about: To know Jesus and to make Him known. In every circumstance—whether we feel like it or not—we are called to light up the world with the "light of the world" (John 8:12). What better way to do that than to give others the opportunity to hear about and trust in Him?

If you'll allow me, I would like to ask you to set this book down for a few moments. When you do, I hope you'll take that time to reflect on this question: What if the above scenario came to fruition in your lifetime?

As you think about that possibility, I hope you'll take comfort in knowing that it's a reality that can actually happen. It can be realized if every follower of Christ does their small part in fulfilling the Great Commission. A task that you may already be doing. If not, that's okay, because one of the goals of this book is to equip you in sharing the gospel with others.

> IN EVERY CIRCUMSTANCE — WHETHER WE FEEL LIKE
> IT OR NOT — WE ARE CALLED TO LIGHT UP THE
> WORLD WITH THE "LIGHT OF THE WORLD."

HELPING OTHERS SEE THE LIGHT

Before we close out this chapter, I want to acknowledge that I'm fully aware that my example is debatable. I wish it wasn't. However, I think it illustrates the importance that you have in helping others see "the light" (see John 1:5, 9:5, 12:35). A truth that the first disciples understood as the Messiah appealed to them. The plea I'm speaking of, is the one Jesus made to His followers. He told them, "The harvest truly is plentiful, but the laborers are few" (Mt. 9:37).

Doesn't that verse make your heart jump? Igniting a flame inside you, to be one of those workers who boldly proclaims the gospel. I believe it does. Especially since you're one of the elite warriors reading this book.

Need more training? Visit **JeffJerina.com** for other self-paced, online courses. For live church or group coaching on evangelism and other key topics visit **JeffJerina.com/Speaking** for availability and options.

CHAPTER 2

SOMETHING WAS MISSING

*Spend more time in study and prayer. That's the secret of
successful evangelism.*
Billy Graham

W hen I first got saved, I had this overwhelming sense of joy. The feeling I had was so intense that I naturally told others about my new life in Jesus Christ. As great as that sounds, I never asked anyone about their personal relationship with the Lord. I, like many others, had been given the greatest gift that anyone could ever receive. One that's meant to be shared with everyone. Yet, I never passed it on. Instead, I left others hanging—wondering how they could have the same hope in Jesus.

I was afraid to ask others about their eternal destination. On the other hand, I had no problem asking someone if they went to church. Although a good conversation starter, a person's response to that question has no bearing on their salvation. Secondly, I had no idea how to accurately present God's redemption plan. Lastly, I failed to comprehend the mandate that Christians have in sharing their faith. Obviously, I was missing something.

What was I lacking? In a word—training.

I honestly didn't know how to present the gospel in a simple and proven manner. However, once I learned what this course will teach you, my witnessing changed. As a result, I've been more confident, better prepared, and more proactive about sharing the gospel. Ultimately, the percentage of people that God has brought to an eternal relationship with Him (through my witnessing encounters) has significantly increased, praise God!

Please understand that I make the preceding statement lightly, as it's the Holy Spirit who wins people to Christ and not us (see Zech. 4:6; 1 Cor. 3:5-9). You and I are simply vessels carrying God's message of love and grace wherever we go. In other words, we are His anointed messengers whom He entrusts to proclaim Christ's victory at Calvary. The apostle Paul writes:

> Now all things are of God, who has reconciled us to Himself through Jesus Christ, and has given us the ministry of reconciliation, that is, that God was in Christ reconciling the world to himself, not imputing their trespasses to them, and has committed to us the word of reconciliation. Now then we are ambassadors for Christ, as though God were making his appeal through us… (2 Cor. 5:18-20).

START WITH THE HEART

If you're wondering if God wants to use you in a similar way, my response is a resounding "YES!" For starters, I firmly believe that God is more interested with your *motive* (or heart) than He is with your earthly resumé. Therefore, I suggest that by reading this book you have a heart for what God wants—which is for *"all men to be saved"* (1 Tim. 2:4). Looking at a well-known biblical figure, I think you'll see my point.

You may recall the story of David's selection as the king of Israel in 1 Samuel 16. It's an account where God repeatedly rejected the candidates that Samuel presented for Saul's replacement until the shepherd boy was introduced. The key text is verse 7, where God told Samuel, "For the Lord does not see as man sees; for man looks at the outward appearance, but the Lord looks at the heart."

I love that verse. It's one of my favorites. It reminds me that God looks at things differently than we do. His focus is on the *internal*, whereas, we spend most of our time concerned with the *external*. To illustrate my point, let's continue our study of David.

Regardless of the sins that David committed, God saw him as a person after His own heart (see Acts 13:22). Even through David's adultery with Bathsheba and the subsequent murder of her husband, God remained more concerned with David's heart (2 Sam. 11-12).[1] Knowing how God saw David in spite of his transgressions, encourages and comforts me in the midst of all my sins.

With that said, I believe your *desire* to want what God wants is the most crucial element in becoming a soul-winner. I say that because we don't always *do* the right thing. But if we *want* to do the right thing, then we allow ourselves to be used by God for His kingdom purposes.

In short, evangelism starts with the heart. More specifically, it starts with the *right* heart. Notice that I didn't say a *perfect* heart. Like David, it's a heart that's *willing* to do the right thing even though you may not always do the right thing.

FINISH WITH PREPARATION

By combining your passion to see others saved with the training in this book, you'll feel more relaxed in your witnessing efforts. In addition, you'll "always be ready to give a defense to everyone who asks you for a reason for the hope that is in you" (1 Pet. 3:15).

Third, you'll have the confidence in knowing that the precepts and steps outlined in this book are biblically based and have proven to be successful in reaching non-Christians.

Fourth, you'll gain a new appreciation for the fact that the Holy Spirit is with you in every witnessing encounter. If you need a reminder of this truth, you can meditate on the promise that Jesus gave the first disciples (see Mt. 10:19-20; Luke 12:11-12).

Finally, each time you share your faith, I believe (at the very least) these things will happen:

- You'll be reminded of how much God loves you.
- You'll sharpen your witnessing skills.
- You'll be more confident in your faith and with sharing it.
- You'll maintain the eternal perspective (see 2 Cor. 4:16-18).

As you move forward in your study of this material, my hope is that you fervently seek the Lord and ask Him to soften the hearts of those you witness to. Likewise, please remember that the power to share the gospel comes from the Holy Spirit. Therefore, we need to humble ourselves in prayer by asking for the Spirit's power to witness. The apostle Paul emphasized this in one of his letters to the church of Corinth. He said,

> And so, it was with me, brothers and sisters. When I came to you, I did not come with eloquence or human wisdom as I proclaimed to you the testimony about God. For I resolved to know nothing while I was with you except Jesus Christ and him crucified. I came to you in weakness with great fear and trembling. My message and my preaching were not with wise and persuasive words, but with a demonstration of the Spirit's power, so that your faith might not rest on human wisdom, but on God's power (1 Cor. 2:1-5, *NIV*).

THE ULTIMATE QUEST

Once you embark on the Great Commission, your life will never be the same. Especially since there's no greater joy (apart from accepting Jesus as your own Lord and Savior) than helping someone else place their faith in Jesus. So, get ready as you start the ultimate quest— setting the captives free.

CHAPTER 3

VICTORY THROUGH CHRIST

But thanks be to God, who gives us the victory through
our Lord Jesus Christ.
1 Corinthians 15:57

F rom the very beginning, God has been on a mission to bring mankind to an everlasting relationship with Him. Knowing that we cannot do this on our own, God's ultimate plan for accomplishing this task came in the form of the Son, Jesus Christ (see John 3:16). The Bible tells us that all who believe in Jesus—and Him alone—will spend eternity in heaven (see John 6:40).

Moreover, the Messiah himself proclaims that He was sent to save the world, despite the sins we've committed (see John 3:15-17). Jesus said in Luke 9:56, "The Son of Man did not come to destroy men's lives but to save them." The apostle Paul reiterates this in Romans 8:1-2:

> There is therefore now no condemnation to those who are in Christ Jesus, who do not walk according to the flesh, but according to the Spirit. For the law of the Spirit of life in Christ Jesus has made [us] free from the law of sin and death.

If you're still not convinced, take a look at what Jesus said in Luke 19:10: "The Son of Man has come to seek and to save that which was lost."

Wow! Did you get that? Jesus actually stepped out of eternity and into our finite world to set us free from the bondage of sin and death. Christ's victory on the cross guarantees that every man, woman, and child who trust in Him will have eternal life (see John 3:16; Acts 16:31; Rom. 10:9). Indeed, Jesus explained this doctrinal truth to His followers.

> And Jesus said to them, "I am the bread of life. He who comes to Me shall never hunger, and he who believes in Me shall never thirst. But I said to you that you have seen Me and yet do not believe. All that the Father gives Me will come to Me, and the one who comes to Me I will by no means cast out. For I have come down from heaven, not to do My own will, but the will of Him who sent Me. This is the will of the Father who sent Me, that of all He has given Me I should lose nothing, but should raise it up at the last day. And this is the will of Him who sent Me, that everyone who sees the Son and believes in Him may have everlasting life; and I will raise him up at the last day (John 6:35-40).

EVERLASTING LIFE

When reflecting on the everlasting life we have in Jesus, I'm reminded how temporal our physical lives really are. Think about it. *Every second, we are all getting older. At some point, we will have taken our last breath on this earth.* It's a fact of life that no one can escape.

But spiritually, each one of us has hope. It's the promise of an eternal home through the blood of Jesus Christ (see Rom. 5:9; Eph. 1:7). A place of residence that we can either accept by our faith in Jesus or reject by trusting in something else for our salvation. And once an individual trusts Jesus as their Savior, God has promised eternal life to each person who does (see John 3:16, 6:40; Acts 16:31).

> CHRIST'S VICTORY ON THE CROSS GUARANTEES THAT EVERY MAN, WOMAN, AND CHILD WHO TRUST IN HIM WILL HAVE ETERNAL LIFE.

Unlike a food item with an expiration date or a vehicle inspection sticker that has to be renewed every year, God didn't save us for a limited period of time. On the contrary, Christ's death, burial, and resurrection guarantees eternal salvation for all those who trust in Him (see John 3:16; Acts 16:31; Rom. 10:9,13; Eph. 1:13; Heb. 7:25; 1 John 5:11-13).

In other words, as a follower of Jesus Christ, you can't lose. You go undefeated in the most important game of all—eternal life. Let that sink in for a few seconds. Christ's sacrifice on the cross wins you and I the ultimate championship—everlasting life with Him in heaven (see John 3:16; 1 Cor. 15:57; Phil. 3:14).

Now before you jump into the first training module (which begins in **Chapter 11**), please take a few moments to read through some actual witnessing encounters. As you go through these real-life accounts, I pray that you'll see at least two things:

- No one is out of God's infinite reach.
- The Father can use anyone to proclaim His name.

Want to be encouraged in your daily walk? **Visit MenUnplugged.net** to hear well-known and inspiring Christian leaders share how Jesus transformed their lives.

CHAPTER 4

SET FREE INDEED

My Testimony

My first job after graduating from college was with a Fortune 500 company. It was a great position with a leader in the telecommunications industry. I had a high paying salary, full benefits, and my favorite—my own business cards.

I can remember thinking: *This is great.* It was the perfect launching pad to begin my career. However, just four months later, my life took a major U-turn.

For starters, I had to get stitches and staples in my scalp and forehead caused from a bar fight I was in. A month later, I totaled my car while driving home late one night. Thankfully, I was the only one involved in the wreck. However, the impact was so strong that my car flipped into the air, broke the windshield and driver's side glass, and caused the left side of my body to skid along the pavement. As a result, I received a severe case of road burn on my left hand.

As if that wasn't enough, I started losing my hair around the same time. Although most people would handle these setbacks in stride, that wasn't the case for me. Unfortunately, I developed a severe form of obsessive-compulsive disorder (OCD)—known as body dysmorphic disorder (BDD). Labeled by some as the 'broken mirror', BDD causes the individual to obsess "about one or more perceived defects or flaws in his or her appearance. A flaw that, to others, is either minor or [unseen]."[1]

That's exactly what happened to me. I constantly thought about every real or perceived defect on my body. The other major symptom of my BDD is the way I looked at these imperfections. In my mind, they would either be skewed or magnified. To put this in perspective, the smallest paper cut seemed like a huge scar on my body (at least to me it did).

I somehow convinced myself that the physical imperfections I had were all that mattered. I thought they defined who I was. Painfully, I felt like I was in this prison made of mirrors that I could never get out of.

Consequently, I wouldn't even go outside without a long sleeve shirt on, and a large bandage covering my hand. Whatever the temperature was—hot or cold—I was wearing long sleeves. But it didn't help. Month after month, I got more and more depressed.

I was so tired of feeling miserable all the time, that the only solution I saw to my happiness was the physical removal of my scars. That was a big mistake! The plastic surgery made my scars significantly worse. As a result, my depression kicked into extreme overdrive.

Eventually my depression got so bad that I thought about ending my life numerous times. The thoughts I had about killing myself went on for a period of four years. The only thing that kept me alive was the fear of going to hell if I committed suicide. I knew I didn't want to go there; however, I couldn't think of another option. By the grace of God, I kept hanging on to what little hope I had.

Following the surgery, I tried secular counseling and psychiatric treatment. Immediately, the psychiatrist placed me on anti-depressant and OCD medications. Regardless of the treatment plan, nothing helped. They only made my symptoms worse.

With no hope in sight, I reached out to my parents for help. Within a matter of days, they had arranged an appointment for me to talk with a Christian counselor. It was here that I discovered the hope and help I desperately needed.

During my second office visit, the counselor told me something that changed my life for good. He shared the gospel with me. Up to that moment in my life (at 30 years old) I had never heard the good news before. For the first time in my life I fully grasped:

- God's infinite and unconditional love for me, regardless of what I thought about myself.
- That Christ's sacrifice paid for my sins once and for all.

It was then that I accepted God's free gift of salvation as I placed my faith in Jesus Christ. There's not a day that goes by that I don't reflect on that moment. Even more so when I share my testimony. To be where I was—without any hope, feeling worthless and unlovable, at the brink of death, to the greatest gift of all—eternal life, is truly a miracle. I know without a shadow of a doubt that Jesus saved my life. He saved me physically and spiritually. He rescued me from the pit that I was in. He healed me of body dysmorphic disorder.

Because of my faith in Jesus Christ, I have an eternal place in heaven. I've been blessed with knowing my best friend and wife, Amy, and I have the honor of being a father to our two children, Kinley and Eli. Thank you, Jesus!

TO LEARN MORE

A PRODIGAL'S JOURNEY

Just so you'll know, I've written a poem (*A Prodigal's Journey*) that highlights my personal testimony. Although it communicates my salvation story, it's written in such a way that anyone can relate to it. You'll find the poem in **Appendix D** of this book. To obtain a copy for your own personal or corporate use, you can purchase the poem in digital format through the following link. The poem is available in two versions (same content) overlaying two different pictures. These versions are a great addition to any room as inspirational wall art.

- The poem is available in PDF format in various sizes at: JeffJerina.com

MY TESTIMONY

If you would like to find out more about my personal testimony, you can do so by:

- Watching a short video of my testimony at: JeffJerina.com/About

- Contacting me for a live keynote or presentation via email: jeff@MenUnplugged.net

Do you need practical tips, biblical wisdom and practical tips from top Christian leaders? **Listen to the Men Unplugged show for FREE at MenUnplugged.net.**

CHAPTER 5

THE POWER OF THE HOLY SPIRIT

Witnessing Story

B efore meeting my wife, I was actively involved with a local singles ministry. During that time, a group of us would play volleyball in the church gym on Tuesday nights. Afterwards, we would go out to grab a bite to eat. However, there was one night in the summer of 2007 when everyone went their separate ways. It was an evening I'll never forget as the events that transpired that night set ripples across eternity. Thus, my story begins.

Just as I was walking out of the fellowship center, I caught a glimpse of someone heading towards me. Upon meeting the gentleman, I found out that he (Kevin) had worked in the church's maintenance department for three years.

While we were chatting, I shared my 30-second testimony with him. After finding out that he was unsure about his salvation, I proceeded to share the gospel. During our hour-long conversation, I told him everything he needed to know to make a faith-based decision.

Nevertheless, he still wasn't convinced that Christ's work at Calvary was enough to save him. Kevin's religious background was firmly rooted in a 'works-based' mentality. His beliefs were so strong that he insisted that his good deeds had to outweigh his bad in order to spend eternity in heaven. Despite all of my efforts, Kevin refused to accept God's grace.

I then recalled a key tenet of evangelism: Our job is not to win people to Jesus; it's only to tell them about Jesus (see 1 Cor. 3:5-7). The Holy Spirit's part is to win people to Christ. In short, our job is to *inform*, and the Spirit's job is to *transform*.

Whew! What a relief. After remembering this fundamental truth, I prayed for Kevin and gave him a gospel tract.

Three weeks later, while I was talking to some friends of mine in the church courtyard, I heard someone yelling at me from a distance. It was Kevin. As he rapidly approached, he was shouting, "Jeff! Jeff! I have something to tell you!"

> OUR JOB IS TO INFORM, AND THE HOLY SPIRIT'S JOB IS TO TRANSFORM.

After catching his breath, Kevin shared an amazing story. He told me that he was unable to go to sleep the night we spoke. Instead, he grabbed the gospel tract I gave him and read it again. This time he read it to himself. While reading the same information I shared with him earlier, he now understood what Christ did for him. As a result, he placed his faith in Jesus. Praise God!

Kevin also mentioned that because he was so excited about his new life in Christ, he woke his wife up that same night. After sharing the gospel with her, she also trusted Jesus Christ as her Lord and Savior that same evening. In addition, he informed me that he and his wife recently got baptized at another church. Since then, they've been serving the Lord faithfully. Hallelujah!

By now, I'm sure you realized what happened. The Holy Spirit won Kevin and his wife to glory. Their salvation experience is a testament of the Spirit's power and how He alone works in the hearts of men and women (John 16:8; 1 Cor. 2:10-11). In addition, their new birth supports a fundamental principle found in Scripture: You and I need the Holy Spirit's power to be effective in evangelism (see Zech. 4:6; Isa. 61:1; Acts 1:8; 1 Thess. 1:5). We cannot do it on our own.

Consequently, their faith-based decision illustrates a basic concept in this course: You and I can't take credit when someone places their faith in Christ, and by the same token we can't take the blame when they don't.

Lastly, I hope you see how this story illustrates the supernatural presence of God through the Holy Spirit when witnessing (see Acts 4:31).

> YOU AND I CAN'T TAKE CREDIT WHEN SOMEONE PLACES THEIR FAITH IN CHRIST, AND BY THE SAME TOKEN WE CAN'T TAKE THE BLAME WHEN THEY DON'T.

Want to be encouraged in your daily walk? **Visit MenUnplugged.net** for valuable resources and to hear well-known and inspiring Christian leaders provide practical tips, biblical truths and valuable wisdom on key topics each week.

CHAPTER 6

ALWAYS BE READY

Witnessing Story

It was December 2014 and I was on the tail end of a stressful Christmas season. Quite possibly the most demanding I've ever had, as my Christmas lighting business was in high gear. Although the Lord has blessed my family with business each year, the last three seasons have really tested my patience. To make matters worse, I was short staffed that year. As a result, I had to perform a majority of the manual labor myself while still juggling all the other roles I had as a business owner. Needless to say, by December I was mentally and physically exhausted.

Just when I thought I was done for the year; I received a text message from a commercial customer of mine. It stated that all of the Christmas lights were out on one of their retail centers. My first thought was: *In the ten years we've installed lights on this building, we've only had two issues.* The second thing I realized was that I hadn't been to this location in almost seven years.

After contemplating whether or not I should take care of the issue myself, I finally decided to head over there. Two hours later, I found myself on top of the shopping center's roof troubleshooting the problem.

Almost immediately, I discovered the source of the outage — the lights were unplugged. Come to find out the owner disconnected the lights a few days earlier. *Great,* I thought, I *could be eating dinner right now with my wife and daughter.* I quickly changed my attitude as I recalled the lesson God taught me the day before (more on that later in this story).

With a renewed outlook, I turned the lights on and noticed that approximately 30 of the 750 incandescent lights were burnt out. *No problem,* I told myself, *this should take about 10 minutes to repair.* Unfortunately, this wasn't the case as many of the bulbs had defective sockets. As a result, it ended up taking two hours to fix.

Finally, at 8 pm I called my wife and told her that I needed to get something to eat before heading home. As I scanned the parking lot from the rooftop, I noticed one of my favorite sandwich shops. With an answer to my growling stomach in sight, I told my wife, *I'm going to get a sandwich.* Luckily, I arrived at the restaurant at 8:22 pm — eight minutes before they closed at 8:30. This was just enough time to order some food. What I didn't know was that God had something more important than a ham sandwich in mind.

While I stood at the counter waiting for two of the three employees to prepare my meal, I began to sense that God wanted me to share my testimony. As one of the gentlemen prepared my sandwich, another one promptly locked the door at 8:30 pm. When he did, I noticed that I was the only customer in the store. After paying for my food, I began to share my salvation story with them. Within minutes, Daniel and Joseph were sitting at one of the tables listening to me share the good news. After hearing the gospel for the first time that night, both Daniel and Joseph placed their faith in Jesus Christ. Hallelujah!

As I reflected on the Spirit's work in bringing these young men to salvation, I couldn't help but be overwhelmed by God's power and timing. I thought about all off the details the Lord had to orchestrate in order for these two gentlemen to hear the gospel that night.

First, my customer had to physically unplug the lights that week as the entire display was operational before then. Second, the odds of getting a service call on this particular property, especially on a Saturday were basically slim to none. Third, the additional time it took for me to repair the lights resulted in my search for food rather than my original plan of eating at home. Finally, the sandwich shop closed thirty minutes earlier on Saturdays than it did on Friday nights. This earlier time gave me the perfect occasion to share the gospel without worrying if I was interfering with their work.

In conclusion, I share this story to illustrate a basic truth concerning evangelism: You and I should always be ready to share the gospel. Looking back on that witnessing encounter, I could have easily chosen to get my sandwich and leave without any mention of the good news. But I didn't. The reason I didn't leave is because I had learned how to communicate my faith through training like this. I was prepared to share God's plan of salvation.

> YOU AND I SHOULD ALWAYS BE READY TO SHARE THE GOSPEL.

CHAPTER 7

A SOURCE OF ENCOURAGEMENT

Witnessing Story

A glimmer of hope. That's the phrase my wife, Amy, used when we were praying one night. It was something that I was losing, quite honestly. For the past several months, I just felt like nothing was happening. I was trying to expand the *Men Unplugged* audience, but it wasn't working. At least, not the way I was expecting. So, Amy—sensing my pain—lifted me up in prayer. She asked the Lord "to show me—in some way—a glimmer of hope."

As great as her prayer was, I really didn't think it was going to do much. Because the reality of the situation, at least what I could physically see, was the growth of the show was moving slower than I wanted. But something happened the next morning that lifted my spirits.

It was one simple email. An email I received from a gentleman who listens to the broadcast. Until that moment, I never knew who he was. Although, it all started to make sense while I read his letter. Joel (the author of the email) informed me that I met his son, Jared, at a daddy-daughter dance that my daughter and I attended. Then it hit me. *I know who Jared is! He's the D.J. I shared the gospel to, after the event was over.* Although Jared was already a saved man, I remember him telling me that he was encouraged by our conversation. To better explain why I'm sharing this story, I've included the email below.

Jeff,

I've listened to several of your podcasts and have been encouraged and challenged by them. What drew me to your show is something that happened back in February (?) of this year.

My youngest son grew up in church and attended Christian schools from day one through high school. He is very smart but always struggled in school. My son became disillusioned about his faith because of the way he was treated by the administration at the school. He dropped out of church and began to explore other religions, as well as, atheism.

In February (I believe) of this year, he was the D.J. at an event you either attended or sponsored. He called us after the event ended and told us that you had shared your faith with him. He was blown away that you would even care about him. He called us after it was over and was shaken. He asked if we thought it was a coincidence. We assured him that God loves him and is pursuing him. His girlfriend is a talented violinist who is in the orchestra at a church in Dallas. My wife told him we all needed to go hear her play the next morning. He tried to get out of going, but my wife is persistent. He reluctantly agreed and we went.

It was your faithfulness to share the good news of Jesus Christ that touched his heart. God has done some amazing things in his life. From one father to another, thank you! Thank you for caring about a young man who felt like Christians do not care about him. Thank you for being willing to take time to speak with him.

I would love to meet you and tell you the rest of the story.

Sincerely, Joel

Wow! What an amazing letter. What do you think I was doing while I was reading that email? I was choking up, for one. At the same time, I was encouraged by Jared's spiritual transformation. I also realized that God answered Amy's prayer. In that one email, my hope was restored.

Reading Joel's letter was uplifting to say the least. Just when I needed a 'glimmer of hope', there it was — an encouraging word from another brother in Christ. I'm honored to say that I had a chance to meet Joel for lunch and hear the rest of the story.

TO GET OTHERS BACK IN THEIR RACE

While we were eating, Joel mentioned that his son hadn't been to church in years. And that it wasn't until my conversation with Jared, that he attended a place of worship again. Now, here's where it gets crazy. As if it hasn't already.

Through a series of events that occurred at Jared's first day back at church, he was able to get a new job, find a church home, and most importantly, he's back in his race. According to his dad, this all happened through that one act of sharing the gospel. There you have it.

That's the golden ticket. It's what we want to hear after sharing Jesus with someone. Especially, in those instances when we don't see an immediate heart change. When — for whatever reason — they don't place their faith in Jesus. Well, at least in that moment we're speaking with them. So, we wonder:

- *Did it matter?*
- *Did, what I share with that person really make an impact?*

If this story is any consolation to you, the answer is an absolute "YES!" It does matter. Although, in some instances you may never know it. But that's okay. Because every time you throw the seeds of the gospel, the greater the chance it's going to sprout up and grow in someone's heart.

Who knows? Your presentation of the gospel could be the first time that person was introduced to Jesus. But for circumstances outside of your control, the individual rejects God's free gift of salvation. But then—months later—something happens in their life and another believer is there to share Jesus again. This time, the individual places their faith in Christ. Although you may never hear about their conversion, the most important things to remember are:

- You were faithful in witnessing.
- Your obedience allowed the individual to hear the gospel.
- The individual placed their faith in Jesus.

EVEN MORE SO

In short, you and I should always be ready to share the hope of Christ with others (see 1 Pet. 3:15; Mark 16:15). By doing so, you can be a *source of encouragement* to anyone you come across (see Col. 4:6).

For the non-believer, you can move them one step closer to a personal relationship with Jesus Christ. Or better yet, to that glorious moment when they place their trust in Jesus Christ.

With respect to fellow believers, your faithfulness in sharing the gospel can encourage others in their daily walk. It can inspire them to share the gospel as well (*see note below*). And as we learned from this account, it can motivate Christians to get back in their own race.

If you have time, you can read how Paul's witnessing efforts encouraged the believers of Philippi to share the gospel with others. Here's a key verse from that passage: "and most of the brethren in the Lord, having become confident by my chains, are much more bold to speak the word without fear" (Phil. 1:14).

CHAPTER 8

JUST ASK

I never learn anything talking.
I only learn things when I ask questions.
Lou Holtz

N ow that you've read through some witnessing opportunities
I've been a part of, I would like to give you a few words of
encouragement. Hopefully, these words will reiterate one of the key
tenets of this book—that you can be *successful* in sharing the gospel.
I say that for a number of reasons, which we'll get to as we move
through this course.

But in this chapter, I want to highlight one specific area. It will
help to setup the remaining chapters, as well as, address what many
Christians have told me they struggle with the most—how to start a
spiritual conversation. To illustrate this point, here's a real-life story.

A QUICK STORY

The tournament director had just given the other coaches and me
some obvious, but disheartening news. He informed us that the
district tennis tournament was being rescheduled for another day. It
was one of those things you really didn't want to hear, but you knew
was coming, especially since it rained that entire morning.

With the news at hand, I rallied the high school team and their parents together for a quick update. As we were packing up to leave the tennis center, one of the parents made an incredible declaration. He said, "Hey, let's go to lunch. I'm buying."

Don't you just love it when someone tells you that? Seriously, those two statements together are hard to turn down.

With a hunger in our bellies and a gracious offer to eat for free, all 30 of us left for the restaurant. After finishing our meals, a few of us hung around the main lobby area to chat.

Between those conversations, I had a chance to talk with a few of the employees. I asked what their names were, how long they had worked there, and how their day was going. During our light-hearted conversation, I asked if they would like to hear how my life turned around for the better. That question is often how I begin sharing my testimony with the hope of proclaiming the gospel.

With the students and parents beside me, one of the hostesses stated that she would like to hear my story. After hearing the entire plan of salvation, the hostess joyfully placed her faith in Jesus Christ. Hallelujah!

We were all ecstatic as we just welcomed a new sister into the body of Christ. As we were getting ready to leave, several of the high school students and parents asked me how I was able to share the gospel in that setting. They genuinely wanted to know how I was able to transition a regular, everyday conversation into a witnessing opportunity.

YOU HAVE THE ANSWER ALREADY

That question—although worded differently at times—is one that I've been asked on numerous occasions. It's one that I had personally thought about as well before I learned how to accurately share the gospel. If you haven't taken my evangelism course or heard me talk about this on the *Men Unplugged* show, you may be wondering the same thing right now. Whatever your reason, let me put your mind at ease, once and for all.

Regardless of how the question is framed, the answer is quite simple. As a matter of fact, the solution to this riddle doesn't come with some exhaustive list of steps that you have to memorize. Nor is there a secret formula you have to get just right. You don't even have to worry about saying a specific set of words or phrases.

On the contrary, you actually have the solution already. It's a simple act of goodwill that you already do. Almost instinctively you do this every time you speak with someone you meet for the first time. Chances are you do this when you're conversing with someone on the phone, at work, the store, the gym, at school, or even in your neighborhood. Okay, so what is it?

You just ask.

Let me say it another way—you just start asking.

When you start a conversation with someone you meet for the first time, you ask that person something about them. You ask a question that shows the individual you care about him or her. Whether it's their name, how they're doing, their job, how their weekend went, or their opinion about some product or service you begin each conversation by asking something about the individual you're speaking with. More than likely, you've never initiated a dialogue with someone you just met by firing off a list of everything about yourself. If you did, that would be pretty weird, right?

With respect to sharing the gospel, this everyday conversational style goes a long way in transitioning a normal conversation into a potential witnessing opportunity. As others sense that you care about them—through the questions you ask—the more they'll be open to the truth that their Creator, God Almighty, loves and cares for them.

Please note that this does not mean that every conversation you have with someone leads to a presentation of the gospel. I wish this wasn't the case. However, I do want to emphasize that by asking questions, your opportunities to share the good news will increase tremendously.

SOME QUESTIONS TO ASK

This could be something as simple as asking the individual if they would like to hear how your life changed for the better. Similar to the way I did in the opening story of this chapter. Some other questions that you can ask, include:

- What do you typically do on weekends?
- Have you ever heard of the word 'gospel'?
- Do you have any spiritual beliefs?
- Have you ever wondered what life is like when we die?
- Do you know that you would go to heaven when you die, or would you have doubts like I did?
- Who is Jesus to you?
- Did I ever tell you how my life changed for good?

Just so you know, we will get into the specifics of how to share the gospel in **Chapter 14: Sharing Your Testimony**. But for now, I want to emphasize that sharing the good news is typically prompted through normal conversation. A give and take between each party. One person asks a question, the other responds. It's something I think you'll find to be true as you apply the principles outlined in this book.

The point I'm trying to make is that sharing your faith is not some robotic act or high-level skill that you need to spend years perfecting. This is not the case at all. It's something that with a little preparation, a good coach (like this book), and a love for others, you can be just as effective at proclaiming the gospel than the most avid evangelist.

ASKING HELPS IN OTHER WAYS

Asking questions not only works in starting a conversation with someone, it also helps in other ways as well. It's a great way to keep the dialogue going when the individual you're speaking to struggles with some aspect of the gospel. Who knows, there may be a question that you ask which helps the person clarify their response even more. You can reply with a Scripture verse, biblical truth or a personal story that will move them one step closer to a faith-based decision.

In the event a non-believer disagrees with you or questions your faith, you can politely and in a 'loving manner' ask them what they believe. Listed below are two questions that you can employ when you're presented with this situation.

- What do you believe?
- Why do you believe that?

As simple as these inquiries are, they get the job done. Each one can help you more clearly understand the individual's belief system (however different or similar it is to yours). Personally speaking, these questions have helped me in my own witnessing efforts.

They are also used by one of my guests on the *Men Unplugged* show. In a 30-minute interview, one of today's top apologists and I discuss some practical ways to defend your faith. If you have time, I would encourage you to listen to that entire interview. I think you'll get a lot out of it. You can access the full conversation (Episode 65) at **MenUnplugged.net/ep65**.

FINAL THOUGHTS

As we wrap up this chapter, my hope is that you see how easy it is to start a spiritual conversation. At the same time, that you are encouraged in knowing that you *already* have the experience, knowledge, and ability to do just that—to transition any discussion into a potentially life changing moment through your presentation of the gospel. Finally, that your willingness to ask questions creates opportunities to—more clearly—understand where someone else is spiritually. Thereby, clearing a path for others to hear and respond to God's free gift of salvation.

Need more help? Visit **JeffJerina.com/Training** for an additional self-paced evangelism course.

For live church or group coaching on evangelism and other key topics visit **JeffJerina.com/Speaking** for availability and options.

CHAPTER 9

HIS MISSION
OUR MANDATE

And He said to them, "Go into all the world and preach
the gospel to every creature."
Mark 16:15

T he overarching theme from Genesis to Revelation is God's never ending quest to bring humanity to an everlasting relationship with Himself. Although He needs no help in doing this, the Great I AM has decided to use ordinary, sinful beings—like you and me—to help complete this monumental task. Jesus reiterates this message, better yet, clarifies it in the Gospels.

The first thing He told the apostles was to "Follow me and I will make you fishers of men" (Mt. 4:19). After His glorious resurrection, He told the disciples, "Peace to you! As the Father has sent me, I also send you" (John 20:21). Jesus' final charge to the disciples was for them to go and preach the good news to everyone; everywhere (see Mt. 28:18-20; Mark 16:15; Acts 1:8).

It would have been one thing for Jesus to issue this directive to His disciples on the basis of who He is—the "Alpha and Omega" (Rev. 1:8). However, the command holds more weight and is more powerful, considering the fact that His main focus and life's work consisted of this singular task. The gospel of Matthew records,

> Jesus went about all the cities and villages, teaching in synagogues, preaching the gospel of the kingdom, and healing every sickness and every disease among the people. (Mt. 9:35).

How cool is that? The only one who has the power to rescue souls was actually winning souls Himself. When considering these and other verses that we'll explore later, we're left with one central mission—to proclaim His name! **So, who has God called to carry out this order? You!**

NO EXPERIENCE NEEDED

Unlike corporate recruitment today, Christ's selection criteria was based on something entirely different. It wasn't based on education, financial status, or previous work experience. Instead, the Messiah chose His 'squad' based on their willingness to follow Him and His core mission of bringing the dead to life. Scripture notes,

> Now when they saw the boldness of Peter and John, and perceived that they were uneducated and untrained men, they marveled. And they realized that they had been with Jesus (Acts 4:13).

The religious leaders were not impressed by Peter and John's gift of gab. Nor were they blown away by their spiritual knowledge. Rather, as I see it, they were amazed how their time with the Lord gave these men the courage to witness.

Regarding the other apostles, Scripture seems to indicate that they had no formal seminary training either. In addition to Peter and

John, two of the other disciples made their living as fishermen as well. This pedestrian 'group of men' were:

> The vanguard of [Christ's] enveloping movement. Through their word He expected others to believe on Him (Jn. 17:20), and these in turn to pass the word along to others, until in time the world might know who He is and what He came to do (John 17:21, 23). His evangelistic strategy—indeed, the fulfillment of His very purpose in coming into the world, dying on the cross, and rising from the grave— depended upon the faithfulness of His chosen disciples to take this task. It did not matter how small the group was … [because] this was the way His Church was to win—through the dedicated lives of those who knew the Savior so well that His Spirit and method constrained them to tell others.[1]

And declare they did!

Upon further analysis of the Old and New Testaments, it's hard to miss the principle that God does great things through ordinary, sinful people. Here's a few that come to mind.

Think about Moses when you think of a normal, sinful individual. Afraid to speak in public, God used him to stand before Pharaoh. A Hebrew by birth, Moses had enough faith and courage to follow God's commands. His obedience led the Israelites out of Egypt's captivity. How about Esther? Here's an orphaned Jewish girl who risked her own life as queen to save her beloved people from extinction. Think about the apostle Paul when you think of a sinner. Once a killer of Christians, Paul finished his life by being the greatest evangelist of all time. Think about Peter—who after denouncing Christ three times—was given the unprecedented honor of leading the Lord's Church.

THE FIRST TRAINING CAMP FOR EVANGELISM

Jesus began His earthly ministry with a training camp for evangelism when he recruited the first disciples (see Mt. 4:18-22). When reading this account, it's essential that we understand the implications of the Lord's question to follow Him at that time.

For starters, some of His first recruits were full-time fishermen. Their entire livelihood was built on catching and selling fish. Like any other profession, it would have required some sort of training to be successful. Who knows? They may have learned the best methods to cast their heavy nets, as well as, the best places to fish.

Matthew Henry notes in his Bible commentary, these men were "poor..., unlearned..., and men [of hard labor]", thus, they "were accustomed to hardships and hazards."[2] As a result of their trade, they were no strangers to managing through life's difficult situations. This—no doubt—is often the case when you decide to step across the front lines of Christ's army and enter into enemy territory by sharing the light of Christ.

So, for them to drop the one thing they knew how to do—that which put food in their bellies—it had to be something that was far more valuable. I often wonder if I would have had the guts to do the same thing. How about you?

Secondly, they were obviously captivated by the presence of the Lord and His mission that they "immediately left" everything they knew in order to follow Him (see Mt. 4:20). When studying this text, it appears that they didn't even go back home to say goodbye to their family and friends.

Are you kidding me? These guys were going away—for who knows how long—and they couldn't even pause to say farewell to their loved ones. They just went. They didn't even take a day or two to consider the pros and cons of what Jesus was asking them to do.

Were these men out of their minds? I guess there are some who would say, "Yes." I, on the other hand, would argue, "No." One reason for my opinion rests on the fact that the disciples recognized who they would be following—the promised Savior of the world (see

John 4:42). Furthermore, I would suggest that they *clearly* understood that Christ's mission to reach the lost trumped every other profession on earth.

WHAT ABOUT US TODAY?

The disciples' three-year journey with Jesus is the greatest adventure any human being has ever traveled. Seriously, these guys literally walked, talked, ate, sat, and served with the Son of God on a daily basis for three years. Their time spent with the Lord and training under His watch gave them the capacity to emphatically proclaim the gospel. But for Christians today, how do we obtain that same evangelistic acumen? The answer to this question can be found in the following chapters.

Need more help? **Visit JeffJerina.com/Training** for an additional self-paced evangelism course.

For live church or group coaching on evangelism and other key topics **visit JeffJerina.com/Speaking** for availability and options.

CHAPTER 10

PRACTICE MAKES PERFECT

Failing to prepare is preparing to fail.
Coach John Wooden

s a former high school athlete, my coaches would emphatically voice the phrase, 'practice makes perfect'. Not something you want to hear as you gasp for breath outside on a tennis court hitting groundstrokes for hours in the blistering Texas heat or in the gym running the same basketball play over and over again until your team executes it properly. Ironically, I now find myself telling my daughter and other athletes I coach those same three words. Why? Because life has taught me: The more you practice something, the better you become at it. Additionally, your comfort level for the skill you're learning increases. The same tenet applies when learning how to share the gospel.

A 120 MPH LESSON

In September of 2000, my dad and I flew to New York for the U.S. Open tennis tournament. Between matches, we had a chance to watch one of the all-time greats, Pete Sampras, warm-up on one of the practice courts. It was amazing to see how consistently and effortlessly he hit his shots. As I watched him crank 120 plus mph serves, I noticed that each ball toss, arm motion, and racquet speed were essentially the same as the one before. Then it dawned on me, Sampras' ability to repeat this action over and over again was linked to the amount of time he spent practicing the fundamentals of a tennis serve. The same principle applies for anything you do in life. Whether it's a sport, a specific skill, a job, or personal evangelism, the adage is true: The more you practice, the better you get.

RIDING A BIKE AND EVANGELISM

Think about the first time you rode your bike without training wheels. If you were like me, you were super excited, but afraid at the same time. You wanted so badly to get those shackles we call training wheels off your bike, so you could be finally be cool. But you still didn't want to face the inevitable—falling down and scraping your knees. As scared as you were and number of times you fell, you kept trying, you kept pedaling, and before you knew it you were riding a bike. Yeah! You were cruising, smiling from ear to ear because you did it. That's what sharing the gospel is like.

The more you prepare, the easier it is to share your faith. When I introduce this principle with others, the response is usually the same. It's like a lightbulb goes off in their head. For the first time, many believers realize that sharing Christ is something they can do as well. It's a skill they can easily learn, regardless of the spiritual gifts, experience, or education they have.

If you've already grasped this concept, that's great! If not, my hope is that by the end of this book you'll fully embrace it in your own efforts to share the gospel. With that said, I would like to ask for your grace in sounding redundant as I continually hammer this point home. In addition, please know the main reason for this emphasis is because we (as the body of Christ) need to hear it. We need to remind one another that each one of us can easily share the hope of Christ with others. We just need to learn how do it.

A LESSON FROM THE GRIDIRON

When I spoke with former NCAA football coach, Dave Rader, about the importance of learning how to share your faith and the benefits of practicing the fundamentals of witnessing, he had this to say:

> In football, there are about eight plays that determine the difference between two evenly matched teams. The thing is, you don't know when those plays are going to come up. So, you have to continually practice those plays to ensure that you're ready. The same thing goes for evangelism. You have to practice over and over again, because you never know when you'll have the opportunity to share the gospel.

To listen to my full interview with Coach Rader, you can do so by going to: **https://MenUnplugged.net/Podcast/Commitment**.

You never know when you'll have the opportunity. You can say that in just about any aspect of life. Whether it's a new business venture that leads to millions in sales, being selected for an award, or sinking a hole-in-one at the golf course; you just never know when those opportunities come up. However, you can increase your chances of success in those moments, the more you prepare and the more you practice the fundamentals of whatever it is you're doing.

THE BASICS OF EVANGELISM

As it relates to evangelism, a believer would—at minimum—need to have some basic understanding of how to communicate their faith. At the core of this knowledge, is learning how to convey the bad news (man's sin problem) and the good news (Christ's solution) to someone else. There are numerous ways to do this, albeit through:

- one verse evangelism (such as John 3:16 or Romans 6:23)
- utilizing Scripture verses to explain the good news/bad news

- the ABCs of salvation (Admit, Believe and Confess)
- the four spiritual laws approach

1. A PLAN

Personally speaking, I'm not a strong proponent of one evangelistic method over the other. However, I am convinced that every born-again believer needs to have at least one template or outline—such as this book—to follow. A witnessing blueprint can:

- increase one's comfort level
- reduce, if not eliminate anxiety
- help the believer stay on course when presenting the plan of salvation

A word of caution: This, or any other book on evangelism is not the ultimate authority on sharing the gospel. That position was, is, and always will be God's Word. The author of Hebrews states,

> The word of God is living and powerful, and sharper than any two-edged sword, piercing even to the division of soul and spirit, and of joints and marrow, and is a discerner of the thoughts and intents of the heart (Heb. 4:12).

Thus, I would recommend that any witnessing technique you decide to use has some element of Scripture in it.

2. YOUR PERSONAL STORY

Another key ingredient in personal evangelism is knowing how to share your testimony. Basically, you need to know how to share what your life was like before you trusted Jesus for salvation and how your life is different now after you've placed your faith in Him. We will cover this in more detail in **Chapter 15**.

3. A JOB PROFILE

Professing Christians need to understand God's role and their part in evangelism. The clarity gained in this area will help relieve the pressure and misplaced burden of bringing others to salvation that many believers carry. If you find yourself carrying this weight, I want to encourage you that help is on the way. In fact, our first and upcoming training module—**Chapter 11: Understanding Your Role in Evangelism**—will put your mind at ease. Personally speaking, the clarity I gained in this module was like an 'aha moment' for me when I started my evangelism training.

Looking back on my first witnessing encounters, I can truly say that understanding both God's role and mine correctly helped me stay relaxed when sharing the gospel. Thereby, ensuring that I didn't place any undue pressure on the listener or myself. As you may recall, the story I shared about Kevin in the first section of this book is a prime example of how important it is to understand both your role and God's task in evangelism. I often wonder how differently Kevin and his wife would have responded—if I forced him to make a decision for Christ—since I held to the notion that it was up to me for their salvation.

4. PROPER MOTIVE

Has anyone ever asked you what your motive for doing something was? Maybe someone asked you why you were being so nice to them. Was it to receive a favor in return? Or were you following the Lord's command to "be kind to one another", because that's what we are called to do (Phil. 2:3-4; John 13:34-35; Gal. 5:22-23)? With respect to sharing the gospel, we need to have the proper motive for telling others about the hope we have in Jesus Christ. So, what should our motive be? How do we maintain it? We study the answers to these questions in **Chapter 12**.

5. POWER

Simply put, Christians need power to proclaim the gospel. This supernatural power, which is given to all believers at the moment of one's salvation, is the Holy Spirit (see Eph. 1:13). Without the divine power of God's Spirit leading the way, our evangelistic efforts would be in vain. Especially since the Spirit is the One who gives you and I the power to witness (see Acts 1:8), as well as, the One who convicts the souls of men and women of their need for Jesus Christ (see John 16:8-11). Moreau et. al notes,

> [The Holy Spirit] ...convicts the world of sin, righteousness, and judgment, [and] ...He ripens fields for harvest, convicting those who do not know Christ, wooing them to commit themselves into His care (Rev. 22:17) and thereby paving the way for evangelistic fruit by means of His invisible work in the hearts of people around the world.[1]

When speaking of the Spirit's power, John Piper states, "... the reason we need it is that without it our witness for Christ will lack deep conviction, self-denying courage, convincing wisdom, and converting effectiveness."[2] I don't know about you, but I sure *need and want* these things when I go knocking on the enemy's door, proclaiming the name of Jesus.

6. PRAYER

Although God's power is readily available to every born-again believer, many Christians miss the opportunity to—fully—tap into it when witnessing. A key reason for this is because they skip the vital component of prayer. Spending time alone—petitioning God—is essential if you want to be effective in evangelism.

For starters, you'll be able to present the gospel with "boldness" (Acts 4:31). Secondly, it will help you maintain the proper motive for sharing your faith. Thirdly, you'll receive the "blessing and support of the Lord" as you remain "in fellowship with Him."[3] Who doesn't want that? Especially when you consider that the battle for one's soul is spiritual rather than physical. This underscores the need for every Christ-follower to humbly ask for the Spirit's hand in proclaiming the gospel message. Lastly, you'll be able to maintain the eternal perspective—which is focusing on those things that matter to God (i.e. reaching the lost) as opposed to the temporal drama of this world that we so often find ourselves worrying about (see 1 Cor. 4:6-8).

Understanding that this issue affects everyone, Paul reminded the church of Ephesus that their 'real battle' is not physical but rather spiritual. The same is true for us today. Paul writes:

> For we do not wrestle against flesh and blood, but against principalities, against powers, against the rulers of the darkness of this age, against spiritual hosts of wickedness in the heavenly places (Eph. 6:12).

A QUICK NOTE

As you begin the first lesson, you'll notice at the end of each module there are three sections to enhance your training:

1. Game Plan section
2. Discussion Questions
3. Personal Challenge section

The **Game Plan** phase consists of a series of actions that will further encourage and equip you in sharing the good news. There will be a box beside each one where you can place a checkmark upon your completion of that item. The **Discussion Questions** can be used as either a personal gauge or to strike up conversations with other believers. The **Challenge** component will encourage you to step out of your comfort zone. Please feel free to work through each one at your own pace. Let's get started!

CHAPTER 11

UNDERSTANDING YOUR ROLE IN EVANGELISM

Lesson 1

*I planted, Apollos watered, but God gave the increase. So
then neither he who plants is anything, nor he who
waters, but God who gives the increase.*
1 Corinthians 3:6-7

We begin these training modules with an explanation of God's part and your job in reaching the lost. In my opinion, this is the perfect place to start as it fosters the proper mindset and motive you need for witnessing. Furthermore, the information you gain in this chapter will help unlock your witnessing potential. As an added bonus, this lesson may help to remove some—if not all—of your fears about witnessing. Personally speaking, my anxieties about sharing the gospel went away after I learned what these roles entailed.

GOD'S PART IN EVANGELISM

Thankfully, the Holy Spirit performs numerous roles in evangelism. Not to mention, the most difficult. In this book, we will be talking about two of those primary functions. They include:

- Empowering believers to witness.
- Winning individuals to a saving faith in Jesus Christ.

If we really wanted to, we could place all of His soul-winning tasks under these two main headings. Let me show you what I mean.

THE FIRST PRIMARY ROLE OF THE HOLY SPIRIT
EMPOWERING BELIEVERS TO WITNESS

With respect to the first role, the Spirit of God emboldens you and I to preach the gospel (see 2 Tim. 4:17; Acts 4:29). He provides the words for us to speak within each of our witnessing encounters. In my opinion, both of these fall under the authority and power that God gives believers to fulfill the Great Commission.

Although the Spirit gives you the words to share, there seems to be a correlation between the amount of time you spend in fellowship with the Almighty (i.e. in prayer and personal Bible study) and the information you are able to receive (i.e. recalling Scripture verses, biblical wisdom, and divine guidance). Consider the following story.

It was Saturday morning and I was just about to take the Scholastic Aptitude Tests (SATs) for my entrance into college. Just saying that makes me cringe. With my number two pencil in hand and the exam paper sealed on my desk, I waited for the test monitor to signal the start of the test. Not because I was ready, but because I just wanted to finish and go home.

To be brutally honest with you, I had not studied much at all for the test, despite constant reminders from my parents to do so. I rationalized my laziness with one excuse after the next. Worse yet, I somehow convinced myself that the honors classes I was taking would be good enough to prepare me for the exam. Man, was I wrong!

Within minutes of the exam, I found myself struggling to answer the questions. As I battled through each section, I couldn't help but think, *What if. What if I would have studied more? What if I would have listened to my parents?* Regardless, I kept pushing through to the end. Finally, the test was over. I left the testing center frustrated and worried, wondering what my grade would be.

Several months later my rude awakening came to fruition as I received my score—a comprehensive total of 920. Yikes! That was not the number I was hoping for. By now, I'm sure you get the point of the story and how it relates to evangelism. You and I need to spend time 'studying' God's Word in order to have the answers for those who are about to hear us 'share' His Word.

Let's get back to the lesson.

Before Christ ascended into Heaven, He told His followers that they would "receive power" to witness "when the Holy Spirit" came upon them (Acts 1:8). One event preceded the other—power before evangelism. In layman's terms: The disciples would not be effective in witnessing apart from the power of the Holy Spirit. A truth that Paul reiterated in his letter to the church of Corinth. He said,

> And so, it was with me, brothers and sisters. When I came to you, I did not come with eloquence or human wisdom as I proclaimed to you the testimony about God. For I resolved to know nothing while I was with you except Jesus Christ and him crucified. I came to you in weakness with great fear and trembling. My message and my preaching were not with wise and persuasive words, but with a demonstration of the Spirit's power, so that your faith might not rest on human wisdom, but on God's power (1 Cor. 2:1-5).

YOU AND I NEED TO SPEND TIME 'STUDYING' GOD'S WORD IN ORDER TO HAVE THE ANSWERS FOR THOSE WHO ARE ABOUT TO HEAR US 'SHARE' HIS WORD.

Without question, Paul had circumstantial evidence to support his statement as he personally witnessed the Spirit's power on more than one occasion. Below are a few examples that come to mind.

Most notably, he experienced the Lord's power during his own conversion on the road to Damascus (Acts 9).

Through the Spirit's power, Paul miraculously healed others both physically and spiritually (Acts 14:8-10, 19:12).

In the town of Eutychus, Paul literally brought a young man back to life (Acts 20:9-12). That's right, from physical death to physical life.

In Ephesus, a number of disciples performed miraculous deeds after Paul anointed them with the Holy Spirit (Acts 19:1-6).

Lastly, Paul's false imprisonment in Rome was a conduit for God's Spirit to empower numerous believers to share the gospel throughout Philippi (Phil. 1:12-18).

We could go on and on with additional examples to support Paul's thesis. However, for simplicity purposes, I hope you will agree that these provide a thorough case.

In support of Paul's claim, the Lord himself declares, "… not by might nor by power, but by my Spirit" (Zech. 4:6). Again, Jesus told the disciples that they "will receive power when the Holy Spirit comes on [them] and [then they] will be my witnesses in Jerusalem, and in all Judea and Samaria, and to the ends of the earth" (Acts 1:8).

Okay, so what does all this mean? Simply put: For the believer, God's part in evangelism is to empower the Christian by His Spirit to witness. Once again: God's part is to empower us by His Spirit.

> ## GOD'S PART IS TO EMPOWER US BY HIS SPIRIT.

THE SECOND PRIMARY ROLE OF THE HOLY SPIRIT
WINNING OTHERS TO JESUS CHRIST

The Spirit of God has another primary role in evangelism. This job, which relates to the non-believer, is the most important one of all. It's the task of winning others to Jesus Christ.

Leading up to this moment in a non-believer's life, the third person of the Triune Godhead paves the way for the individual to understand the good news (Acts 14:27; Col. 4:3). Once that person is attuned to the things of God, the Spirit then pricks the heart of the listener by helping them understand Christ's redeeming work (Acts 16:14). Finally, the Spirit of God convicts the sinner of his or her need for Jesus Christ so they can make a faith-based decision (John 16:8). In so doing, God has removed the burden of leading others to Christ from you and I so that we can focus on our one and only job.

> GOD'S PART IS TO BRING OTHERS TO SALVATION.

YOUR PART IN SHARING THE GOSPEL

If God's role in evangelism is to empower his followers to share the gospel and win others to Christ, then what's your charge? The answer to this question is found in the second chapter of Peter.

> But in your hearts revere Christ as Lord. Always be prepared to give an answer to everyone who asks you to give the reason for the hope that you have. But do this with gentleness and respect (1 Peter 3:15).

Your part in evangelism is to be prepared. That's it. Nothing more, nothing less.

> YOUR PART IS TO **BE PREPARED.**

Some biblical translations use the word 'ready' for 'prepared'. The idea being that: No matter what one's education, background, vocation, or spiritual maturity is, a believer should be ready at any given moment to tell others about the life saving message of Jesus Christ. Especially when you consider that there is "so much at stake."[1] What hangs in the balance is the eternal salvation of another human being. Now, this statement is not meant to put pressure on you or any other believer to share the good news. Rather, it's a reminder that you and I should 'be prepared' to share the hope that we have with others. By doing so, we won't miss an opportunity to impact the life of someone else.

In a way, evangelicals serve as Christ's messengers. You and I are agents of God who have been tasked with the honor of preaching the good news to anyone we meet. Paul's exhortation to the Corinthian church emphasizes this point.

> Now all things are of God, who has reconciled us to Himself through Jesus Christ, and has given us the ministry of reconciliation... Now then, we are ambassadors for Christ, as though God were pleading through us... (2 Cor. 5:18, 20).

NEVER CONFUSE YOUR PART WITH GOD'S PART IN REACHING THE LOST.

In clarifying these verses, my good friend and a mentor of mine, Brad Strand, notes that "every believer is called to the ministry of 'reconciliation' (i.e. witnessing for Christ - 1 Pet. 3:15) [and that] we are called to be 'ambassadors for Christ' (Mt. 28:18-20)."[2] The *Jesus Film Project* has this to say about Paul's charge to the Corinthian believers and us today,

It's God's desire that the world would submit to be reconciled to Him, and He is making that appeal through us, the church. We are the diplomats that God has sent to represent Him in this foreign territory.[3]

THE HOLY SPIRIT'S ROLE - A BIBLICAL EXAMPLE

The story of the Ethiopian eunuch coming to salvation in Acts 8 illustrates the dynamic relationship between the Holy Spirit and a professing believer in evangelism. With regards to the role of the Holy Spirit, we see the divine influence the Spirit had before, during, and after this encounter. I've listed several ways below:

1. **The Holy Spirit was responsible for leading Philip to the Ethiopian's location;** thereby, giving Philip the opportunity to testify (verse 26). In the same way, the Spirit guides modern day believers to those who need to hear the gospel today.

2. **The Spirit of God opened the door at exactly the right moment** for Philip to initiate a spiritual conversation (verse 29). Without the Spirit's prompting, Philip may have never known that the Ethiopian man was reading a passage out of Isaiah (verse 30), thereby, indicating a potential need to hear the gospel (verse 31).

3. **Through the power of the Holy Spirit, Philip was given the words to respond**—to the eunuch's questions—concerning salvation (verses 30-37; Luke 12:12). Because the Spirit has been with you from the moment of your spiritual birth, the same power has been at your disposal as well (see Rom. 8:9-11, 16; 1 Cor. 6:19; Eph. 1:13). All you have to do is ask for it (see Luke 11:13).

4. After the Ethiopian received Christ's free gift of salvation, **the Spirit supernaturally directed Philip to his next witnessing encounter** (verses 39-40). At first glance, the abrupt nature of Philip's visit seems out of sorts. Especially since the eunuch (who is now a new believer) is left to decipher God's Word on his own. However, when you look at the meeting through eternal lenses you learn that:

    o   Our *initial* focus should be on creating disciples first, because a person has to *become* a disciple before they can ever *mature* as one. The way we do that is by giving others a chance to have the same hope we have, through our verbal presentation of the gospel (see Rom. 10:14-15).

    o   There are more captives to set free (see Luke 10:2).

5. **The Holy Spirit knows when a person is ready to be discipled.** Over and over again, I have to remind myself of this simple truth: Our task in witnessing is to *plant the seed, not inspect it.* I wonder if this was God's final point here—to remind us that He, our Heavenly Father, knows when, how, and the right time to deal with His children; better than we do. Therefore, we have no reason to get frustrated or feel guilty when we think a new brother or sister in Christ misses an opportunity to be discipled.

YOUR ROLE - A BIBLICAL EXAMPLE

Equally important is the role that Philip played in the Ethiopian's conversion. Listed below are five elements about Philip's obedience that you and I can practice today. When followed, we will be doing our part in fulfilling the Great Commission.

1. **This passage emphasizes the need for believers to "be prepared" at any given moment to proclaim the good news of Jesus Christ** (verse 35). Although we don't know the exact reasons why God selected Philip for this encounter, we can surmise from the text that Philip was ready to witness (vv. 30-37).

2. By being prepared, **Philip understood that he did not have to add anything to the gospel.** He simply shared God's Word (verses 35-37); trusting in the Holy Spirit to do the hard work of conversion. As you advance through this course, you will understand that Scripture is your best tool for reaching the lost.

3. **Philip's actions illustrate a key component of evangelism. They demonstrate how evangelicals need to rely on the Holy Spirit for the power to witness.** On more than one occasion we see how Philip's willingness to follow the Spirit's directions paved the way for the gospel to be heard. Philip's actions are a vivid reminder that soul-winners need the Spirit's power to be effective in evangelism.

4. **Philip's actions serve as an example that you and I need to have an 'eternal intent' when sharing our faith.** When studying verses 28-30, we see that Philip acted promptly. As soon as the Spirit told him to go, he went. When the Holy Spirit told him to talk to the eunuch, he didn't waste a second. He ran over there because he knew that if God wanted him to speak to that man, the Lord had a divine appointment for him (verse 30). In other words, God had an eternal destination for that gentleman, and it's called heaven. Because Philip had an 'eternal perspective', he cut right to the

chase (verse 30). Philip's first question was one of a spiritual nature, indicating that he had an 'eternal intent' (verse 30). As Christ's ambassadors, you and I need to have this same quickness today.

5. **Philip's witnessing encounter took place in the normal ebb and flow of life.** As the eunuch was going about his day reading a passage from Isaiah, Philip encountered him on the dirt road from Jerusalem to Gaza. There wasn't any planning or a formal appointment that Philip had to make in order to speak to the Ethiopian. Rather, his evangelistic encounter took place in the spur of the moment, initiated and guided by the Holy Spirit. Thus, you and I need to be willing to stop what we are doing for the sake of the gospel as well.

LESSON WRAP-UP

As we wrap up this first lesson, remember that God's two-part role in evangelism is to: 1) **empower** Christians by His Spirit to witness, and 2) to **win** souls for Jesus Christ.

Our part is to be ready to share His life saving message to those we come across. Before you advance to the next lesson, take a few moments to work through the **Game Plan** section alone or with your small group. Lastly, consider taking the **Personal Challenge** at the end of this chapter.

Do you need additional training for yourself, your organization, school, or church? **Visit JeffJerina.com to connect with me for workshops, online courses, live training, and more.**

GAME PLAN

- ❑ Pray (ask) for the Holy Spirit's power to share the gospel to someone this week.
- ❑ Remind yourself of God's role and your role in evangelism. *Note: You may want to create a daily reminder via an email or your electronic calendar to help jog your memory.*
- ❑ Read Acts 8:26-40.
- ❑ Discuss the following questions with your small group or another believer.

DISCUSSION QUESTIONS

1. Before reading this module, what did you think God's role in evangelism was?
2. What did you think your part in evangelism was?
3. When was the last time you shared the gospel?
   1. Who did you share it with?
   2. What was the result of your conversation?
   3. What has been keeping you from witnessing?
4. What observations did you make from Acts 8:26-40?

PERSONAL CHALLENGE

I got the idea for this challenge from Bruce Wilkinson's book, *The Prayer of Jabez*. Every time I take this 40-day challenge I'm amazed how many doors God opens to share the good news. I pray the Lord will provide you with a surplus of witnessing opportunities as well.

Here's the challenge: For 40 days pray this prayer from 1 Chronicles 4:10: "Oh, that You would bless me indeed, and enlarge my territory, that Your hand would be with me, and that You would keep me from evil, that I may not cause pain!"[4]

CHAPTER 12

THE PROPER MOTIVE

Lesson 2

We love because he first loved us.
1 John 4:19

I n the previous section, we defined what God's role and your part in evangelism is. Now that you have a clear understanding of these specific functions and who performs each one, it's important to address the issue of 'motive' as it pertains to evangelism. The reason we do that is because your motive for sharing the gospel sets the pulse for your witnessing efforts.

A proper motive will energize and embolden your personal evangelism. It can help you stay ready to proclaim the name of Jesus Christ (see 1 Pet. 3:15). At the same time, it will help you maintain the eternal perspective—which is focusing on the eternal rather than the temporal (see 2 Cor. 4:16-18).

On the other hand, an improper motive will seem laborious and unfulfilling. This type of motive can take the excitement out of sharing Jesus with others. And worse yet, it can rob you of the joy you should have when hearing about or seeing another person place their faith in Christ.

Hence, the reason for *why* you share the gospel matters. Below are some *faulty reasons* for professing your faith:

- You want to check it off your 'to do' list.
- You feel pressured by others to do so.
- You want to be recognized or noticed by others.

Here's a list of *proper* motives for sharing your faith.

- You want others to have everlasting life (see Rom. 10:14-15).
- You love others (1 Peter 4:8; Jude 22-23; Mark 12:31).
- You want to obey God's call to evangelize (Mt. 28:18-20; Mark 16:15).
- As a result of your witnessing efforts, you want to encourage others to do the same (Phil. 1:12-18; 3 John 3).
- It strengthens your relationship with God (see Philem. 5-6).
- Your motive for preaching the gospel is based on Christ's love for you[1] and His mission to reach the lost.[2]

In 2 Corinthians 5:14-15, Paul reminds us that our reason for serving God should be based on 'His love for us' rather than 'our love for Him'. The point here is that our emotions are often short lived, fickle, and unstable (to say the least). However, God's love is unconditional, unchanging, and everlasting. When thinking about it that way, we should have no other reason for sharing the gospel. Reason being, we know in the deep recesses of our soul that the Creator of the universe loves us no matter what, forever!

Equipped with an understanding of God's role, your task, and the right motive for witnessing, we now come to the most exciting part of this book—learning how to share the gospel. Join me as we continue this training in the next lesson: **Overcoming Obstacles**.

GAME PLAN

❑ Pray (ask) for the proper motive to share your faith.

❑ Confess to God any improper motives you may have or once had about witnessing.

❑ Read Romans 8:38-39 and 2 Corinthians 5:14-15.

❑ Discuss the following questions with someone else or your small group.

DISCUSSION QUESTIONS

1. What should your main focus be in witnessing?

2. Armed with the knowledge of God's infinite love, how does that impact your motive for sharing the gospel? Explain.

3. Read Philippians 1:12-18 and then discuss Paul's reason for his statement in verse 18.

4. After you've had a chance to witness to somebody—regardless of whether or not they accepted Christ as their Savior—how can you edify another believer?

PERSONAL CHALLENGE

Write down the names of those (you know) who have shared the gospel with someone this year. Pray for their protection, provision and the Holy Spirit's power to witness again.

1. _____

2. _____

3. _____

CHAPTER 13

OVERCOMING OBSTACLES

Lesson 3

*For God has not given us a spirit of fear, but of power and
of love and of a sound mind.*
2 Timothy 1:7

One of my favorite vacation spots is Santa Rosa, Florida. It's a place where my family and I go to relax and unplug from the normal stressors of life. My routine is typically the same every morning we are there. I wake up at 5:30, get ready, pick up my Bible and foldable lawn chair, and then I'm out the door. After a five-minute walk to the beach, I arrive—the best part of my day.

With my feet in the sand, sitting by the shore, I look out into the ocean and admire God's creation. For 30 minutes, it's just me in the presence of my Abba Father. That's pretty much how it goes every morning.

Notice that I said, *pretty much.*

The first day I went to the beach was a bit different. Yes, I arrived around the same time. I even had the same Bible and foldable lawn chair. For the most part, I sat in the same spot watching the waves crash along the shore line. But then it happened. As I was praying for an opportunity to share God's love to someone who needed to hear it, I heard something behind me. It was a young man that was putting up beach chairs and umbrellas. He wasn't just setting up two or three. It was more like 30 or 40.

Realizing this was an answer to my prayer, I walked over to where he was and introduced myself. During our conversation, he mentioned that he owned a beach rental company. Although he had a lot of equipment to setup, he really wasn't moving that fast. I mean, come on... it's the beach, right?

So, I shared my testimony and asked him if he would like to know how he could have the same hope I have. His first response was that he's an atheist (let's call this Obstacle 1). Then he said he didn't have the time (let's call this Obstacle 2). I thought, *why would God have me come over here after I just prayed, if He didn't want me to at least share the gospel with this gentleman.* Then it hit me. *How about asking Sean if I could help him setup the chairs and umbrellas. And I will offer to do it for free, if he listens to me share the good news.*

He agreed. So, that's what I did. While I was helping him setup the beach furniture, Sean listened as I shared the gospel with him. Although he didn't trust Jesus as his Lord and Savior, he heard the gospel for the first time that day.

Was it worth it? Was my hard work, sweat, and time worth Sean hearing the gospel that morning? Definitely! It was worth it because the gospel was planted in his heart (see 1 Cor. 3:6). Now it's up to the Holy Spirit to do the rest.

A DIFFERENT OUTCOME

You may be wondering why I shared this story. Especially since the gentleman I spoke to, did not make a faith-based decision. At least, not that I know of. I mention this encounter for a couple of reasons. First, it's important to acknowledge that not every opportunity you have to share the gospel *will* lead to a salvation. At least, not in that moment. However, the individual can make a faith-based decision hours later (like Kevin did in **Chapter 5**). It could be days, months, or even years after you spoke to the person. Regardless of the outcome, the best that you and I can do is our part—*be ready* to share the hope of Christ with others.

OBSTACLES CAN BE OVERCOME

The other reason I share this story is to illustrate the main focus of this chapter—that obstacles can be overcome. In my conversation with Sean, I could have easily left without sharing the good news. But I pressed on and saw those obstacles as what they are—just hurdles. Although they may present some problems, they're not permanent structures or force fields that can never be breached.

On the contrary, obstacles can quickly and easily be conquered. At times, it may require some creative thinking on your part (similar to me offering to help Sean out for free). Other times, it can be a simple change of location or a request to follow-up with the individual at another time. For instance, you could move to a different table or room if the ambient noise prevents the individual from hearing your presentation of the gospel. Personally speaking, I've had to do this numerous times, and it helped. Thus, it's my belief that whatever the obstacle is, it can be overcome.

THE BIGGEST OBSTACLE

Webster's dictionary defines an obstacle as "something that makes it difficult to do something…"[1] When it comes to preaching the gospel, the biggest obstacle that many Christians face is fear. However, Paul reminds us that "God has not given us a spirit of fear, but of power and of love and of a sound mind" (2 Tim. 1:7).

In addition to giving us the Spirit's power to witness, He assures His followers that He will provide the words to speak during each encounter (see Luke 12:11-12, 21:15).

If the Almighty gives believers the power to evangelize and the words to speak, then why do so many evangelicals fear sharing their faith with others? In my opinion, it's two-fold. For starters, these individuals have never been trained how to accurately share the gospel. Second, most Christians—me included at one point in my life—place the burden of winning people to Christ on themselves rather than where it belongs—the Holy Spirit.

COMMON FEARS ABOUT WITNESSING

Listed below are some reasons why many believers find it difficult to share their faith. They think or say:

- I don't know how to start a spiritual conversation.
- I don't know that much about the Bible.
- I don't feel like I'm qualified enough.
- I'm afraid that I'll do more harm than good.
- I'm afraid of being rejected.
- I don't want my friends to think I'm judging them.
- What if they ask me something, I don't know the answer to?

Other barriers include such things as: Time, a lack of giftedness in evangelism, or interpersonal skills. However, these difficulties are lessened when a Christian recognizes that it's not his or her job to win someone to Christ, which is a key point we covered in Lesson 1.

GIVE CREDIT WHERE CREDIT IS DUE

Furthermore, as we discussed in the chapter titled, **His Mission Our Mandate**, Jesus took twelve ordinary men who had little or no prior education and literally used them to transform the world. Their success in spreading the gospel—despite their lack of education and religious background—gives hope for all of us. This hope is evident to every disciple of Christ, regardless of your upbringing, giftedness, or spiritual maturity. Why is that? Because ultimately, it's God who does the supernatural work of conversion. Paul's letter to the Corinthian believers says it best:

> Who then is Paul, and who is Apollos, but ministers through whom you believed, as the Lord gave to each one? I planted, Apollos watered, but God gave the increase. So then neither he who plants is anything, nor he who waters, but God who gives the increase. Now he who plants and he who waters are one, and each one will receive his own reward according to his own labor. For we are God's fellow workers; you are God's field, you are God's building (1 Cor. 3:5-9).

The apostle's words in 1 Corinthians 2:3-5 cut to the crux of the whole matter. His exhortation reminds believers that people do not come to faith by human actions or words. Instead, individuals come to experience God's free gift of salvation through the gospel alone. Or as Paul states, through the "power of God" (Rom. 1:16). First Corinthians 2:3-5 says:

> I came to you in weakness with great fear and trembling. My message and my preaching were not with wise and persuasive words, but with a demonstration of the Spirit's power, so that your faith might not rest on human wisdom, but on God's power.

The role of a believer—as we learned in Lesson 1—is to *be ready* to give others the information needed to make a faith-based decision. That's it. Nothing more... Nothing less... Just be prepared! This readiness—I might add—includes the willingness to do so.

Paul reminded the church in Rome that, "The goodness of God leads you to repentance" (Rom. 2:4). Notice that it doesn't say 'our goodness'. It specifically states, God's benevolence!

In the gospel of John, Jesus told the crowd that gathered around Him, "No one can come to [Him] unless the Father who sent [Him] draws them, and [He] will raise them up at the last day" (John 6:44).

Consequently, when someone places their faith in Jesus Christ, you and I cannot take the credit as though it were something that happened by our own words or actions. In the same way, we can't take the blame or feel like we failed in witnessing when they don't.

> IT'S NOT YOUR JOB TO WIN OTHERS TO CHRIST; IT'S YOUR JOB TO TELL OTHERS ABOUT CHRIST!

NO PRESSURE

Thus, you and I have *no pressure* in evangelism other than being *ready* to give an account for the reason we believe. Let me say that another way. Because the Holy Spirit alone convicts the hearts of men and women, neither you nor I should carry the burden of winning people to Christ. As a result, most—if not all—of your fears about witnessing should be remediated because all of the hard work is performed by God. If you're like me, this realization will feel like a massive weight has just been lifted off your shoulders.

In short, being prepared to share the gospel is far less confrontational and combative when you have this mindset. Reason being, you won't feel like you have to convince or win someone to Christ. Not to mention, it's much easier and less burdensome to do. Personally speaking, I become frustrated and tired when I have to persuade or argue with someone to make my point clear. However, when I simply relay the facts without the pressure of gaining their approval or persuading them to see my point of view, I'm more relaxed. How about you?

This brings me back to one of the stories I shared in the **Victory Through Christ** section. As you may recall, I mentioned a particular instance when I spoke to a gentleman by the name of Kevin. In that lengthy conversation, I simply shared the gospel message without placing any undue stress on him to accept Jesus as his Lord and Savior. Instead, I remembered that my role as Christ's ambassador is to be willing and ready to proclaim the good news and allow the Holy Spirit to perform the supernatural part of conversion. By understanding my task and God's part in evangelism, Kevin and his wife placed their faith in Jesus by the work of Holy Spirt and not me. Glory to God!

THREE POINTS TO REMEMBER

Before you work through the **Game Plan** section in this chapter, I want to emphasize three points that will help you overcome those witnessing obstacles. First and foremost, it's not your job to win others to a saving knowledge of Jesus Christ. Second, it's only your job to tell others about Him (see Ezek. 3:17-19; Mt. 28:18-20; Rom. 10:14-15, 17). Third, neither you nor I can convince someone to believe in God, whom they cannot physically see or touch. Only the Creator can do that. In short, it's only your job to *inform* and the Holy Spirit's task to *transform*.

GAME PLAN

☐ Pray (ask) for the Holy Spirit's power to share the gospel to someone this week (see Luke 11:13).

☐ Confess (to God) any fears you might have about witnessing.

☐ Read Romans 10:1-17.

☐ Discuss the following questions with your small group and/or another believer.

DISCUSSION QUESTIONS

1. Of the common fears listed above, which one—if any—do you struggle with the most? Why?

2. What other fears do you have about sharing the gospel?

3. Has this lesson helped in remediating any fears you may have about witnessing? Explain.

4. From your study of Romans 10:1-17, how does verse 15 make you feel when thinking about evangelism?

5. From your study of Romans 10, have verses 14 and 17 confirmed your definition of evangelism or have they changed it? Explain.

PERSONAL CHALLENGE

Write down on a sheet of paper all of the fears that you have (or once had) about sharing your faith. Pray over each one asking the Lord to take them from you and replace them with the courage and power to share the gospel.

CHAPTER 14

FIVE STEPS OF WITNESSING

Lesson 4

Everyone, who calls on the name of the Lord will be saved.
How, then, can they call on the one they have not believed
in? And how can they believe in the one of whom they
have not heard? And how can they hear without someone
preaching to them?
Romans 10:13-14

S haring the gospel is one of the most rewarding experiences that you'll ever have. It has the potential to impact the life of another human being for good; for all eternity. Within seconds, the Holy Spirit can take your words and supernaturally change the heart of the listener—in such a way—that they fully grasp and accept God's free gift of salvation through their faith in Jesus.

With that said, I often hear fellow believers express their interest in learning how to defend their faith. Which is awesome by the way. It truly is. Especially when you understand their reason: They want to make sure the answers they give about Christianity are accurate. However, I scratch my head when some of those same Christians state that they've never learned how to present the plan of salvation.

The reason I make this statement is because the order of their preparation or what they want to learn first is reversed.

Hence, I believe it's imperative that you learn how to share your faith *before* you actually know how to defend it. In other words, you can't defend your faith until you first know how to share it.

It's like putting the cart before the horse. It doesn't work. Now, please don't get me wrong here. I'm not saying that we shouldn't know how to do the work of apologetics (i.e. the defending of our faith). Rather, by understanding how to share the good news your foundation for the defense of the gospel is much stronger.

In addition, you'll be more effective in your witnessing efforts. This is something that world-renowned apologist and author, Josh McDowell, mentioned in one of his books. When having to write a graduate paper on "The Best Defense of Christianity", Josh opened with this statement:[1]

> 'Some people say the best offense is a good defense, but I say to you that the best defense is a good offense.' I proceeded by explaining that I felt the best defense of Christianity is a 'clear, simple presentation of the claims of Christ and who He is, in the power of the Holy Spirit.'[2]

RESOURCES TO HELP YOU DEFEND

Before we move on with this lesson, I wanted to provide you with some information that can help you with apologetics. It's a series of interviews that I've had with several Christian apologists on the Men Unplugged show. Each one is a great addition to the training in this book. You can listen to each interview at **MenUnplugged.net** by typing the word 'apologist' in the search bar.

One of those conversations was with Josh McDowell, whom I mentioned above. When you get the chance, I would encourage you to listen to that podcast (Episode 50). It's a 33-minute masterclass where Josh provides wisdom on a variety of topics. For your convenience, here's the link: **MenUnplugged.net/Episode50**.

> # YOU CAN'T DEFEND YOUR FAITH UNTIL YOU FIRST KNOW HOW TO SHARE IT.

So, there it is. Sharing the hope of Jesus with others really is that simple. It can be easy and straightforward because you can learn how to share the gospel. Thus, it's up to you to *be ready*. Part of that preparation is understanding the steps involved in presenting the plan of salvation.

FIVE STEPS OF WITNESSING

There are essentially five steps to sharing the gospel. Hopefully—with the Lord's help—the third, fourth and fifth stages are reached. As you think about these steps, one thing to keep in mind is that every witnessing opportunity you have is different than the next. Not to mention, these steps happen organically as you're presenting the plan of salvation. In other words, they just flow from one phase to the next.

But for simplicity purposes, it's a good idea to know what stage you're in while you're witnessing to others. By doing so, you'll know where you've been and where you need to go in your presentation of the gospel. It reminds me of my time as a waiter in college and a concept called 'windows.' Similar to the five steps of evangelism, this is a restaurant's tool that helps servers manage their tables. In their version, waitstaff have four windows of serving (drinks, appetizers, entrées, and desserts). And it was your job as a server to know what window you were in at each table. Let me tell you, it made things so much easier. At least for me it did.

The last thing to know about these evangelism steps is that their order is not set in stone. You may find that in some instances you can skip over one or more of these phases. Other times, sharing a verse like John 3:16 or Romans 6:23 is all that's needed for someone to place their faith in Jesus Christ. Regardless, understanding these steps and knowing what to do in each one will simplify your witnessing efforts. They will also help by taking the guesswork and fear out of sharing the gospel. Listed below is an outline of the phases involved:

- **Step 1:** Share Your Testimony
- **Step 2:** Trust Statement
- **Step 3:** Gospel Presentation
- **Step 4:** Drawing the Net
- **Step 5:** Assurance of Salvation

A QUICK NOTE REGARDING THE THIRD STEP

As you approach **Chapter 17** (Lesson 7), you'll notice that I've split this stage (Step 3) into two lessons. Although, both lessons go hand-in-hand, it's been my experience that splitting them into separate modules is easier to follow and practice. Other than simplicity, some other reasons for doing this are as follows:

- to help you with your explanation of the term 'gospel' when witnessing
- to better explain the transition statement between the *Trust Statement* (Step 2) and this stage in the gospel presentation

A QUICK NOTE ABOUT THE FOURTH STEP

The Sinner's Prayer is a tool that helps a new believer understand and confirm their profession of faith. It is not required for salvation. However, I think it's a good idea to go through it, if time allows. Who knows? The Sinner's Prayer may be the first time the new Christian has ever prayed. Regardless of whether or not you lead a person through the Sinner's Prayer, the most important aspect of Step 4 is the individual's profession of faith (through their understanding of the gospel message).

ON DISCIPLESHIP

It's important to note that just because someone is a new believer, it does not mean that they're ready to begin the process of discipleship or what is known as the maturing of one's faith. Understanding this fundamental principle will help alleviate any anxiety you may have about witnessing, especially when you're speaking with someone you may never see or converse with again.

Do you remember the story of Philip the evangelist and the Ethiopian eunuch in Acts 8? As you may recall, there wasn't any discipling that took place between Philip and the eunuch. In short, God knows better than you and me when an individual is ready to be discipled. Therefore, we don't have to feel pressured to get a person into church, a Bible study, or the baptistry right away. God has that figured out already. He knows when to do all this in His 'best' timing and His 'best' way.

Please don't misunderstand me here. I'm not implying that God wants us to stop equipping others in their Christian walk. More importantly, I'm not even suggesting He's disinterested with the spiritual growth of a new believer. On the contrary, what I'm saying is that this burden—which is often carried by evangelicals—is not a requirement for evangelism, nor is it essential.

I share this section on discipleship because it was something that helped me personally in my own witnessing efforts. It took the 'burden' of teaching someone how to mature in their faith off of me and placed it where it should be—on the Holy Spirit. This understanding gave me the freedom to simply share how Jesus Christ radically changed my life—through His work on the cross—and how others can have that same hope. I pray you experience this same freedom in sharing the gospel as well.

GAME PLAN

❑ Pray (ask) for the courage to share the gospel with others.

❑ Write the five steps of sharing your faith in a place that you access on a regular basis (i.e. your Bible, phone, computer, etc.).

❑ Complete the discussion questions by yourself or within a small group.

DISCUSSION QUESTIONS

1. Which of the five steps interest you the most? Explain.
2. Which of the five steps do you think will be the toughest for you?
3. After reading the section on discipleship in this chapter, how has it changed—if any—your thoughts about witnessing?

PERSONAL CHALLENGE

List the names of three people you plan on sharing the gospel with.

1. _____
2. _____
3. _____

Need more help? Visit **JeffJerina.com/Training** for self-paced, additional evangelism training. For live church or group coaching on evangelism and other key topics visit **JeffJerina.com/Speaking** for availability and options.

CHAPTER 15

SHARING YOUR TESTIMONY

Lesson 5

Sing to the Lord, bless His name; Proclaim the good news

of His salvation from day to day. Declare His glory among

the nations,His wonders among all peoples. For the Lord

is great and greatly to be praised…

Psalm 96:2-4

It was a beautiful October day in Texas. The sun was shining. The sky was blue, and the temperature was just right. It was the perfect day to play golf, go to the park, or just sit outside and admire God's creation. While I was running errands, I found myself at a hardware store buying a new ladder rack for my truck. After I purchased the item, one of the workers helped me carry it out to my vehicle.

As we walked to my truck, I shared my personal testimony with him. I soon found out that my salvation story was enough to peak the gentleman's curiosity about the gospel. After we loaded the ladder rack into the bed of my truck, I asked if he would like to know how he could have the same hope that I have. He responded, "Yes I would, especially after hearing your story."

With his permission, I shared the good news through the method outlined in this course. Upon asking him if he would like to accept God's free gift of salvation, he emphatically said, "Yes!" After trusting Jesus as his Lord and Savior, he then shared with me that hearing how God changed my life, gave him hope for his.

YOUR STORY MATTERS

The point I'm trying to make is that your testimony matters. It's significant just the way it happened. Nothing added. Nothing taken away. Furthermore, your salvation story is a crucial element in presenting the gospel. For you—it's the intersection of your life before and after you placed your faith in Jesus Christ. With respect to the individual you're sharing it with, it's an authentic and personal account of God's love and grace in your life.

Your personal testimony brings the all-powerful and invisible God to a real and visible person (you) that they can see, touch, and communicate with. Thereby, giving the individual hope that God cares for and loves them as well. In other words, the individual who hears your story learns how your life has been radically transformed by the same Messiah you're telling them about.

As you may recall, the Bible states in Romans 2:4, "The goodness of God leads [people] to repentance." Therefore, it's imperative that others hear how benevolent and loving He is. In addition to the reasons above, here are some extra benefits for sharing your personal testimony.

- Your testimony acts as a bridge to the gospel message itself.
- The individual who hears your testimony will quite often find some facet of your story that they can relate to as well.
- Your transparency about your life will naturally encourage

the listener to be more forthcoming about theirs.

- You'll be reminded how much your heavenly Father loves you as you reflect on your own salvation experience.

BE WILLING TO ADAPT

Please note that this outline is simply a template to assist you in sharing your testimony. Feel free to modify your affidavit to best fit your salvation experience. There may be instances where you will need to adapt your personal testimony to the person or people group that you have a chance to share it with.

Author A. Scott Moreau points out that Paul's willingness to *adapt* "the message based on the audience" is a valuable lesson in helping Christians "avoid building unnecessary obstacles" in conveying the good news to others.[1]

Your ability to adapt your salvation story to the individuals you witness to will help expand your outreach potential. Notice the key word here is the verb 'adapt'. It does not mean alter or change. Practically speaking, you may find that certain parts of your testimony affect others differently. For example, if you know the individual has a works-based mentality and this was your belief system at one time, it would help that person understand God's free gift of salvation better knowing that you can relate with them. As such, you'll want to include this in your testimony. This is obviously easier to do the more you know the individual. However, it's not entirely impossible to convey in those situations when you don't.

Let me explain.

When you share something 'real' about yourself with another individual, the chance of them opening up about an aspect of their life increases as well. I guess it's human nature. This idea of give and take. Personally speaking, I'm more transparent with others—about my life—the more candid they are with me about theirs. With respect to evangelism, your personal story creates the environment for this interaction to occur. And when it does, you can help the non-believer take one step closer to Jesus.

ANY TESTIMONY WILL DO

The brother of one of my former seminary professors, Dr. Vernon Whaley, notes that "testimony is… a fourteenth-century Anglo-French word, from the Latin testimonium, meaning 'evidence,' or 'witness.' It's a firsthand authentication of an event, an open acknowledgment of what one has experienced, seen, heard, felt, enjoyed, or endured."[2] Therefore, as a personal account of how God changed your life it's essential that you communicate your testimony to the world, regardless of however mundane or dramatic you think your conversion was.

Right now, you may be thinking your testimony isn't that great. You may have this idea that personal testimonies are only effective for individuals with an extreme salvation experience. Someone like a former drug addict, an individual rescued from a tough childhood, or a person who placed their faith in Jesus after a life-threatening accident. Although this may seem to be a valid concern, it's irrelevant when presenting the good news. Reason being: Every born-again believer has one thing in common. This prevailing thread is the uncertainty of one's salvation that we all had until we individually trusted in Jesus Christ alone for our salvation. It doesn't matter if your life was radically transformed as an adult or with childlike faith as an adolescent.

The point to remember is that your testimony is powerful just the way it happened—nothing added or taken away. I like the way Brennan Manning puts it. He says,

> Our impulse to tell the salvation story arises from listening to the heartbeat of the risen Jesus within us. Telling the story does not require that we become ordained ministers or

flamboyant street corner preachers, nor does it demand that we try to convert people by concussion with one sledgehammer blow of the Bible after another. It simply means we share with others what our lives used to be like, what happened when we met Jesus, and what our lives are like now.[3]

YOUR TESTIMONY IS POWERFUL JUST THE WAY IT HAPPENED—NOTHING ADDED OR TAKEN AWAY.

THREE THINGS TO SHARE

When giving your testimony, you'll want to communicate three things. These items will help you relate to the unsaved individual on a real and personal level. Additionally, they're a springboard to the gospel message itself. It's also important to note that they apply to each and every believer.

Therefore, it doesn't matter what your age was when you trusted Jesus Christ as your Lord and Savior. By the same token, it doesn't matter what your spiritual maturity level is now or what your life was like before you placed your faith in Jesus. With that said, you'll want to include these items in your testimony:

- **There was a point in your life when you doubted that your salvation was secure.** This is the moment you realized that you needed and confessed your need for and trusted in Christ as Lord and Savior. In short, it's a brief explanation of your life before your faith-based decision.
- **What were the circumstances that led you to a saving knowledge of Jesus Christ?** This may include details such as: The individual who shared the gospel with you, where you were when you got saved, how was your life before

Christ, and what was your biggest trial or struggle.

- **How is your life different since placing your faith in Jesus?** This doesn't have to be explained in full detail. However, it's important to share how God has made your life better.

COACH'S TIP

Before you share the gospel with others, it's a good idea to have a 30-second and one-minute testimony that you've already written out and practiced. This early preparation will help you stay relaxed and equipped so you can communicate more effectively. When relaying the three points above, try to focus on your eternal security and the positive impact Christ has made on your life rather than a detailed record of your conversion.

SAMPLE TESTIMONIES

Listed below are five examples of how you can share your testimony. You'll notice that the focus is not on a lengthy account of how you came to faith. Rather, it's a short hop from your testimony to finding out where the individual you're speaking to is spiritually, or in this book, the *Trust Statement*.

As you'll see in the next chapter, obtaining a person's *Trust Statement* is paramount in understanding their spiritual beliefs. It also helps in presenting the good news itself. Hence, you'll want to have some type of question at the end of your testimony where you ask the person if they know whether or not they're saved. A question like: *Do you know for sure that you would go to heaven when you die, or would you have doubts like I did?* When you ask this type of question, you're creating a bridge between your salvation story and what the listener believes is required for eternal life.

Before you review and practice these examples, let me highlight something about this chapter and the next five (Lessons 6 - 10). In these chapters, you'll learn a step-by-step method for sharing the gospel that I've used and teach since 2005. Hopefully, you find this approach as a simple and practical guide for sharing the good news. For your convenience, each lesson provides a list of the questions and statements in this method and an explanation of each module.

To accelerate your training, I recommend you role-play these lessons with someone else. You can do that by going through the outline version of this method—located in **Appendix A**—in the back of the book. It contains the entire plan of salvation mentioned in these six lessons.

NOTE:

In order to make the reading of these examples easier, I'm leaving the quotes off of each question or statement. Also, please note the following acronyms that we will be using in each lesson.

WB = Witnessing Believer (individual sharing the gospel)
LP = Lost Person (individual you're sharing the gospel to)

EXAMPLE 1:

WB: Someone asked me (a while back) if I knew that I would go to heaven when I die or if I would have doubts.

WB: I wasn't really sure.

WB: They shared something with me that helped me understand how I could know for sure I was going to heaven.

WB: Let me ask you, if you were to die today, would you be 100% sure that you would go to heaven or would you have doubts like I did?

EXAMPLE 2:

WB: About <u>18 years</u> ago, my life changed for the better.

WB: <u>Someone</u> shared something with me that <u>changed</u> my life.

WB: They asked me if I was sure that I'd go to heaven.

WB: I honestly didn't know.

WB: If I could ask you the same thing, do you know for sure that you would go to heaven or would you have doubts like I did?

Fill in the underlined words above to match your testimony.

WB: Would you like to know for sure?

If the LP says YES, then begin asking questions from Lesson 6.

EXAMPLE 3:

WB: Do you have any spiritual beliefs?

WB: For a while, I didn't have any. But then something happened.

WB: When I was _____ years old, my life changed for the better.

Fill in the blank above to match your testimony.

WB: Someone asked me if I knew whether or not I was 100% sure that I would go to heaven when I die.

WB: I really didn't know how to answer that question.

WB: I knew I did some good things… but at the same time, I've done a lot of bad things as well.

WB: So, I said, "I really don't know."

WB: If I could ask you the same thing: Do you know for sure that you'd go to heaven, or would you have doubts like I did?

WB: If you have a few minutes, I'd like to share with you—how you can know for sure?

If the LP says YES, then begin asking questions from Lesson 6.

EXAMPLE 4:

WB: Have you ever heard of the gospel?

WB: Do you know what it is?

Note: Regardless of whether or not the person tells you Yes or No, I would encourage you to share it with them anyway. By doing so, you may find that their definition of the gospel is incorrect.

WB: I use to think it was Matthew, Mark, Luke, and John. These are actually the first four books of the New Testament.

WB: However, what I learned was that these are the gospels (plural), that help to explain the gospel (singular).

WB: The Gospels include the gospel, but only the gospel gets you to heaven (Romans 1:16).

WB: Would you like to know what the gospel is?

EXAMPLE 5:

WB: Have you ever known anyone that was <u>severely depressed</u>?
Note: Fill in the blank above to match your testimony. This can be any question that relates to your personal story of salvation?

WB: I struggled with <u>severe depression</u> for <u>4 years</u> of my life.

WB: I had <u>suicide thoughts almost every day</u> until someone shared something that <u>turned my life</u> around.

WB: They told me how I could know for sure that I'd go to heaven.

WB: Ever since then, my life has changed for the better—<u>no more depression, no more need for anti-depressants, or counseling.</u>
Note: You'll want to fill in the underlined words above with your own salvation story?

WB: How about you, do you know that you would go to heaven when you die, or would you have doubts like I did?

WB: If you have a few minutes, I could tell you how you can know for sure.

30 AND 60-SECOND TESTIMONIES

Just in case you need a creative boost, I've included my personal 30 and 60-second testimonies below. If I had to guess which of these I use more often, I would have to lean towards the 60-second version. Reason being, it's been my experience that most people are generally interested in hearing how someone's life has turned around for the better. Thus, a longer testimony gives the listener a more detailed account of how Jesus Christ improved your life.

MY 30-SECOND TESTIMONY

My life is so much different now than it was 18 years ago. Back then I was severely depressed. I had suicidal thoughts almost every day for a period of four years. And then someone shared something with me that saved my life. They told me about the gospel of Jesus Christ. That He died, was buried, and rose again on the third day. And because I was unsure that I would go to heaven when I die, all that I had to do was trust in Jesus Christ for my salvation. How about you? Do you know that you would go to heaven when you die, or would you have doubts like I did?

MY 60-SECOND TESTIMONY

Nineteen years ago (at the age of 30) I was struggling to stay alive. From the ages of 26 to 30, I was severely depressed with suicidal thoughts every day of my life. Although I was taking antidepressant medication and going to psychiatric counseling, nothing helped. To make matters worse, I felt like an ugly duckling. I thought there was no way God could ever love me because of all the bad things I had done.

Out of desperation I went to a Christian counselor. He asked me if I knew I would go to heaven when I died. After telling him about all of the terrible things I did, I told him I would have doubts. He told me about the gospel of Jesus Christ, that Jesus' death on the cross paid the price for my sins, and that all I had to do was accept God's free gift of salvation by faith in Jesus Christ alone. Since then, I've finally been able to look at myself in the mirror and be happy with who I am. More importantly, I know that my salvation is secure.

If I could take a Bible and show you how you can know for sure you're going to heaven when you die, would you be willing to consider it?

LESSON WRAP-UP

I hope this lesson has helped you create your 30 and 60-second testimonies. Please remember that these are just templates and, as such, may not fit your personality or communication style. On that note, sometimes I just ask the individual if they know who Jesus is. Other times, I simply ask if they've ever heard of the gospel or what the gospel means. Regardless of the questions you ask, I recommend that you do it with the right motive rather than as a laborious task that you have to check off your 'to-do' list.

Before you move on to the next chapter, I want to encourage you to go through the **Game Plan** section and discussion questions at the end of this chapter. They will help you develop and practice sharing your testimony. In addition, it's great training for the next chapter.

Want to be encouraged in your daily walk? **Visit MenUnplugged.net** for valuable resources and to hear well-known and inspiring Christian leaders provide practical tips, biblical truths and valuable wisdom on key topics each week.

GAME PLAN

- ❑ Pray for the words you would like to share in your testimony.
- ❑ Write out your 30 and 60-second testimonies on a sheet of paper. *If it's easier, feel free to type them on your phone or your computer.*
- ❑ Practice sharing each testimony to one or more individuals this week (preferably other Christians at this point).
- ❑ If you're in a small group, discuss the following questions with one another.

DISCUSSION QUESTIONS

1. Why is sharing your testimony so important in evangelism?
2. When is the last time you shared your testimony? Explain?
3. What is the most memorable part of your testimony?

PERSONAL CHALLENGE

Make an audio or video recording of your 30 and 60-second testimonies. Replay the recording to see how natural you sound.

Need help in writing your testimony? **Visit JeffJerina.com to learn more about my coaching, online courses, seminars, and virtual or live keynotes that are tailored to help you share your story with others.** While there you can schedule a FREE 15 minute discovery call with me at JeffJerina.com/Contact.

CHAPTER 16

THE TRUST STATEMENT

Lesson 6

*If you confess with your mouth the Lord Jesus and believe
in your heart that God has raised Him from the dead, you
will be saved.*

Romans 10:9

B y now you're probably wondering what the *Trust Statement* is
and how this stage fits in with the other phases of sharing your
faith. The *Trust Statement* helps the professing Christian understand
what another individual believes is needed for salvation. Rather than
asking questions that have no bearing on a person's eternal life (i.e.
if they go to church or what they do on Sundays) the *Trust Statement*
requires the listener to provide a definitive answer to the most
important question of all: Are they saved?

On a personal note, the biggest advantage that I've experienced
with this witnessing tool is that it helps me clearly understand what
the individual's beliefs are about salvation. As you'll see, the *Trust
Statement* invites the person to state what they specifically believe is
the requirement—or requirements are—for going to heaven. Thus, it
helps you understand the next step you need to take in your
witnessing encounter.

So how do you implement this tool in your efforts to share the gospel? Listed below is a breakdown of the steps to take, as well as a few real-life examples that you can practice alone or within your study group (if you're in one) . If you still need more training with this stage, I think you'll find the role-playing section helpful. It can be found in **Appendix A** in the back of this book. I also offer an online course that you can take at **JeffJerina.com/Courses**. That course, as well as, my group training will enhance the principles you learn throughout this book. Alright, let's see the *Trust Statement* in action!

TRUST STATEMENT STEPS (THE DELIVERY)

- **Step 1:** Share your personal testimony.
  *See **Chapter 15** for more help.*
- **Step 2:** Ask a question similar to:
  - o Are you sure that you're going to heaven when you die? Or would you have doubts, like I did?
- **Steps 3 and 4:** See Table 1 at the end of this chapter.

At this point in the *Trust Statement*, the individual whom you're witnessing to will more than likely respond with one of several statements. Although their reply may not be exactly as the ones listed below, the idea will essentially be the same. While you're waiting for their answer, it's a good idea to pray silently for the Holy Spirit to open their hearts to the gospel.

POSSIBLE RESPONSES YOU MAY RECEIVE FROM STEP 2

- **Response 1:** They think they deserve to go to hell.
- **Response 2:** They deserve or sure they're going to heaven.
- **Response 3:** They're unsure.
- **Response 4:** They don't have any spiritual beliefs.
- **Response 5:** They don't want to talk about this right now.

HOW TO RESPOND TO THE LOST PERSON'S REPLY

At the end of this chapter, you'll find **Table 1**. It includes a list of replies that you can respond with in relation to each of the five responses above. Before viewing that table, please keep in mind that your replies do not have to be verbatim. However, I would suggest that the focus of your question is similar to the ones listed as it will help you get to the presentation of the gospel quicker. This is where the real heart transformation begins—hearing the Word of God (see Heb. 4:12; Rom. 10:17).

With respect to *Response 1* above, you'll want to ask for the individual's permission to present the plan of salvation. Possible ways to do that are found in the second column of **Table 1**. If the lost person answers "Yes" to your reply, you'll want to ask follow-up questions similar to the ones provided in *Step 3 of the Trust Statement.* That step and corresponding questions are outlined in **Table 1.**

The reason you'll want to ask these questions is to understand what the potential convert is really basing their salvation on. In so doing, you may discover that this individual is placing their salvation in something other than faith in Christ alone.

But what if the lost person replies with a negative statement like "No" or "I'm not interested." What do you do then? In this situation, you'll want to ask if you can give them a gospel tract, a Bible or a link to the Men Unplugged page, so they have a way of hearing or seeing the words of the gospel. Examples of how you can do that are listed in the third column of *Response 4* under the column: *WB Next Step to Take.*

For *Responses 2 and 3*, proceed to *Step 3 of the Trust Statement stage.* Similar to *Response 1*, the questions to ask the individual you're witnessing to are listed in **Table 1.**

For *Response 4*, it's a good idea to ask for permission to share the gospel. If the individual is still reluctant to hear the good news, you might want to give them a gospel tract or a New Testament Bible, if they don't already have one.

For *Response 5*, I would ask for their permission to follow up at a later date. If so, you can ask for their business card, phone number or email address. You might consider giving them a gospel tract.

Hopefully, you can see how effective the *Trust Statement* stage is in helping you understand what a non-believer thinks the requirements are for salvation. Often times—in this stage—you'll find that the individual is already a born-again believer. Which is great news! However, the person may doubt that his or her salvation is secure.

Without speculating on the reason for their doubts, I want to encourage you that at this point you have a divine opportunity to remediate their uncertainty. Because you've used the *Trust Statement*, you can erase their doubts once and for all by sharing a few Scripture verses. These verses will help them understand that their salvation is eternally secure. Two of my favorites are Ephesians 1:13 and Hebrews 7:25.

WHAT'S THE GOAL?

The goal that you're trying to reach in obtaining the lost person's *Trust Statement* is to **determine what they believe is needed for salvation.** Some people will tell you *they're already saved*. Others will say *they're good to go*. However, after probing deeper into their answers, I've often discovered that their basis for salvation is something other than their faith in Jesus. Some believe they deserve to go to heaven by what they do—such as works. Others have the opinion that they're saved by their faith in God plus the good deeds they perform—which is grace plus works. In short, we can never assume an individual is saved until that person agrees that:

1. He or she is a sinner.
2. Their sin separates them from God.

3. Jesus Christ is God.
4. Jesus died for their sins, was buried, and rose again.
5. Jesus is the only one who can save them.

Therefore, you can fill in the blank of *Question 2* in the *Trust Statement's* third step with several items. For example, you might say, "I could go on and on with a list of things that you feel is necessary for salvation, but the point that you, LP, are making is that there are at least two or three things that you would have to do."

On occasion, I'll say something else to transition to the next step of the gospel presentation. Here's an example of what you might say, "I had those same thoughts for years and then I heard the gospel and it changed my life. That's what I'd like to share with you now."

Want to be encouraged in your daily walk? **Visit JeffJerina.com** for valuable resources and to hear well-known and inspiring Christian leaders provide practical tips, biblical truths and valuable wisdom on key topics each week.

Table 1: How to Respond to the Lost Person's (LP) Reply

LP Response	WB (your) Reply	WB Next Step to Take
Response 1	Ask one of these questions:	"YES" reply:
	Would you mind if I shared with you how my life was changed?	If the Individual (LP) responds to your reply with "YES" go to Step 3 of **Trust Statement**
	Do you mind if I take five minutes to share the gospel with you, what actually saved my life?	"NO" reply: Proceed to Next Step to Take in Response 4 below
Response 2		Proceed to Step 3
Response 3		Proceed to Step 3
Response 4	You can ask for permission to share the gospel. Similar to your (WB) reply to Response 1 above. Or take the next step for this response.	You can give the LP a gospel tract. Or ask for their number to follow-up. Or send them to this page: MenUnplugged.net/Gospel.
Step 3 of Trust Statement	**Question 1:** What do you think you would have to do in order to go to heaven? **Question 2:** How about _____, would that help? *Fill in the blank above with the following phrases:* * Doing good things * Being king to your neighbor * Keeping the commandments * Going to church * Obeying your parents	Proceed to Step 4 of the **Trust Statement**
Step 4 of Trust Statement	You can say something like: So basically, you're depending on several things to get you to heaven. Is that right?	Proceed to STEP 3 of **Witnessing** (Sharing the Gospel - Lesson 7)

GAME PLAN

- ❑ Pray (ask) for the Holy Spirit's power to share the gospel.
- ❑ Practice the *Trust Statement* scenarios with someone else this week. It's a good idea to do this face-to-face and over the phone for additional practice.
- ❑ Role-play your 30-second testimony in Lesson 5 together with this *Trust Statement* step with someone else this week. Use **Table 1** in this chapter along with **Appendix A** in the back of the book for help role playing the WB and LP.
- ❑ Create in your own words a short response for each of the LP's responses above.
- ❑ Discuss the following questions with your small group or another believer.

DISCUSSION QUESTIONS

1. Why is the *Trust Statement* so important when sharing the gospel?
2. Why do you think Christians stop short of asking an individual the reasons why he or she believes they're going to heaven?
3. What's another item you can think of to fill in the blank in Step 3 of the *Trust Statement*?

PERSONAL CHALLENGE

Write the names of those you know who are non-believers. Place an asterisk next to the individuals whom you have known longer than three years. Pray that the Lord will open their hearts to the gospel and that He will provide you or someone else the opportunity to share the good news with them.

CHAPTER 17

SHARING THE GOSPEL

Lesson 7

For Christ did not send me to baptize, but to preach the gospel, not with wisdom of words, lest the cross of Christ should be made of no effect. For the message of the cross is foolishness to those who are perishing, but to us who are being saved it is the power of God.
1 Corinthians 1:17-18

For most of my life, I had no idea what the gospel was. I thought it was the first four books of the New Testament. It wasn't until I heard an accurate presentation of the gospel that I understood what it truly is.

Today, many people have the same belief. Others think something entirely different. Whatever their precepts are, these misunderstandings about the gospel are inaccurate. These fallacies can act like walls blocking someone from accepting God's free gift of salvation. In your efforts to share God's love with others, you'll want to remove these barriers as quickly as you can. So, how do you do that?

Now that you're in the third step of sharing your faith, you'll want to—first and foremost—explain what the gospel actually is.

The best way to do this is through Scripture. Utilizing God's Word is crucial in presenting the gospel message accurately, since it's His Word that needs to be heard and not ours. Consider what the author of Hebrews writes:

> For the word of God is living and powerful, and sharper than any two-edged sword, piercing even to the division of soul and spirit, and of joints and marrow, and is a discerner of the thoughts and intents of the heart (Heb. 4:12).

The first verse I recommend sharing is Romans 1:16. It clearly states what the gospel is. When you start with this verse, you'll be helping the non-believer understand why he or she needs to hear the message itself. For training purposes, I've provided a brief outline on how you can start the gospel presentation below. Remember 'WB' is for 'witnessing believer' (you) and 'LP' is for 'lost person' (the person you're witnessing to).

SHARING THE GOSPEL (OUTLINE)

WB: Romans 1:16 states that "The gospel is the power of God to salvation for everyone who believes…"

WB: The word **'gospel'** means **good news**.
This statement helps the non-believer understand what you're saying the gospel is—which is the good news of salvation.

WB: When we translate the gospel into the original language the New Testament was written in, Greek, the actual definition is 'good news'.

WB: But in order to appreciate the good news we have to understand the bad news first. The bad news is something about all of us.
This is your transitional statement. It bridges the definition of the gospel into the Bad News portion of the presentation. Anyone who is about to hear the bad news will want to know that there's good news just around the corner.

NOTE:

Similar to the previous chapter, a role-playing section is available for this lesson—in **Appendix A**—at the back of the book. In addition, I offer an online training course that you can take at your own pace. It's available at **JeffJerina.com/Courses**. That course, as well as, my group training will enhance the principles you learn throughout this book.

For a **FREE handheld version** of this outline and subsequent lessons, turn to **Appendix C** of this book. That chapter introduces the **Pocket Gospel** which you can download for FREE as the owner of this book. It can be downloaded at **JeffJerina.com/Books/FaithWithoutFear/PocketGospel.**

GAME PLAN

❏ Pray for opportunities to share the plan of salvation with others.

❏ Practice memorizing Romans 1:16.

❏ Practice saying, "The gospel means good news."

❏ Highlight Romans 1:16 in your Bible.

I think you'll find that a small handheld Bible works best as you can have it available at all times. When I first started sharing the gospel, I had a pocket-sized New Testament Bible that I kept in my back pocket.

❏ Role-play this lesson with someone else you know. It's a good idea to do this face-to-face and over the phone for additional practice.

❏ Practice your testimony (30 or 60-second version), the *Trust Statement* and this lesson with someone else this week.

DISCUSSION QUESTIONS

1. Is this definition of the gospel different or the same as you once believed?

2. In your opinion, why do you think so many others have an incorrect view of the gospel?

3. Do you think this step will help you present the gospel more accurately? Explain.

PERSONAL CHALLENGE

Ask a family member, friend, co-worker, or neighbor if they know what the gospel is. If they do, politely ask them to share it with you. You may be surprised to find out that they don't know. Use this question as an opportunity to explain the gospel as it's defined in Romans 1:16.

CHAPTER 18

SHARING THE BAD AND GOOD NEWS

Lesson 8

*For the wages of sin is death, but the gift of God is
eternal life in Christ Jesus our Lord.*
Romans 6:23

N ow that you've explained what the gospel is, you'll want to
shift gears and describe the bad news—man's problem of sin
and the penalty for it. In so doing, you'll help the non-Christian
understand his or her need for Jesus. That's under the precept that
they fully accept their sin condition and God's remedy for it. Before
we continue, I want to pause for a quick pointer.

COACH'S TIP

As best as you can, be relaxed and talk naturally without feeling as
though you have to say everything exactly the way I've outlined in
these modules. Remember that sharing your faith is not some
'robotic act' or calculated speech that you have to memorize. It's a
divine opportunity to share God's love and message of hope with
another human being. Therefore, it's a good idea to let:

- the Holy Spirit guide your words
- Scripture be your voice
- Jesus Christ sell Himself
- The Father to provide you with the opportunities to witness

I truly believe that as you do these things, sharing the hope of Christ will no longer seem as a mundane task that you have to plow through. Rather, it will be one that you enjoy being a part of and are passionate about doing.

> IN EVERY WITNESSING ENCOUNTER YOU HAVE, I ENCOURAGE YOU TO LET THE HOLY SPIRIT GUIDE YOUR WORDS...SCRIPTURE BE YOUR VOICE...JESUS CHRIST SELL HIMSELF... AND GOD THE FATHER PROVIDE YOU WITH THE OPPORTUNITIES!

SHARING THE BAD NEWS

Have you ever known anyone that liked hearing bad news? Of course not. As great as your day may be going, hearing subpar news—especially if it relates to you—is no picnic at all. In some cases, the information you hear can ruin your entire week, if not year. However, the upside to sharing the bad news of the gospel presentation is that it ends with the greatest hope of all—victory in Jesus Christ. Therefore, telling someone the bad news with this finish line in mind will help you and the lost person as you begin this step.

The following outline is a simple and proven template to use during your witnessing encounters. Feel free to add verses to it as the Spirit leads you. The central verses in this bad news section are:

- Romans 3:23
- Romans 6:23

- Revelation 20:14-15

You may also want to use:

- Romans 3:10 in conjunction with Romans 3:23
- Luke 12:4-5 to support the passage in Revelation

BAD NEWS OUTLINE

Whenever you see the verse written out, you can either verbally share it with the individual listening or have them read it aloud from your Bible or gospel tract.

Verse 1: Romans 3:23
"For all have sinned and fall short of the glory of God."

WB: All of us have done, thought or said something wrong at one point in our life. Even a lie that you tell your parents when you were growing up is a sin.

WB: I've told a few lies before. How about you?

LP: Yes, all of us have.
Note: The individual you're witnessing to may say something different. However, for our purpose here, we'll use this response.

WB: In the Bible, this wrong action—even a tiny lie— is called sin.

WB: Because of this sin we have to realize that we miss God's mark of perfection (as the Bible states, the glory of God) meaning that we are all sinners.

WB: But the bad news gets worse.

Verse 2: Romans 6:23
"For the wages of sin is death..."

WB: The Bibles says that the wages or payment for just one sin is death. Not just physical but spiritual death.

WB: As such, the Bible states: A person's soul must face a spiritual death or what the Bible calls the second death, unless their sins are paid for.

<u>Verse 3:</u> **Revelation 20:14-15**

"Then death and Hades were thrown into the lake of fire. The lake of fire is the second death. Anyone whose name was not found written in the book of life was thrown into the lake of fire."

WB: <u>LP</u>, just as the bad news got worse the good news gets even better.

COACH'S TIP ON REVELATION 20:14-15

You may sense that paraphrasing this passage would be easier for the non-believer to understand. If so, here's what I often share with others: "The Bible states in Revelation 20:14-15 and I'll paraphrase, when we die a physical death and our sin (even just one) is not paid for, then we experience a second death which is eternal separation from God. In other words, rather than spending eternity with God in heaven we deserve to go to hell."

SHARING THE GOOD NEWS

You've now reached the phase of the gospel presentation where you explain the good news of the gospel! In my opinion, this is one of the most exciting parts of evangelism. Just think, the verses you proclaim here are ones that breathe life and hope into the individuals you speak with. The core verses in this segment are:

- Romans 5:8

- 1 Corinthians 15:3-4
- Ephesians 2:8-9
- Romans 10:13

Other Scripture verses to consider are:

- John 3:16, 14:6, 4:25-26, and 5:24
- Romans 10:9

Please remember that whenever you see the verse written out, you can either verbally share it with the individual listening or have them read it out loud from a Bible or gospel tract.

GOOD NEWS OUTLINE

WB: That's the Bad News. Now comes the good news!
This transitional statement is central in helping your presentation flow seamlessly from the bad news to the good news.

Optional: You could say, "Just as the bad news got worse the good news gets even better."

Verse 1: Romans 5:8
"God demonstrates his own love for us, in that while we were still sinners, Christ died for us."

WB: What this verse is telling us is that God meets you and I where we are right now. Regardless of whatever bad or good we may have done. He gives us the ultimate solution to our problem of sin through the work of Jesus Christ. Let me explain.

Verse 2: 1 Corinthians 15:3-4
"... Christ died for our sins according to the Scriptures, and that

> He was buried, and that He rose again the third day according to the Scriptures."

WB: Jesus Christ died on a cross, was buried, and rose again on the third day proving that He is, was, and always will be God.

WB: His sacrifice paid for all of your sins—past, present, and future.

COACH'S TIP ON 1 CORINTHIANS 15:3-4

In an effort to shorten this passage and aid in memorization, you may want to paraphrase it as follows: Jesus Christ died, was buried, and on the third day He rose again. Also, feel free to share this verse along with Romans 1:16 when communicating the definition of the gospel in **Chapter 17.**

> <u>Verse 3:</u> **Ephesians 2:8-9**
> "For it is by grace you have been saved, through faith—and this is not from yourselves, it is the gift of God - not by works, so that no one can boast."

COACH'S TIP ON EPHESIANS 2:8-9

This passage in Ephesians provides an opportunity to more clearly describe the gospel message. Listed below are a few suggestions you can implement when sharing the plan of salvation with others.

WB: Did you know that the word 'grace' here means undeserved favor? In other words, you and I were given something we don't deserve - a full pardon for our sins.

WB: What's even better is that you and I were given this apart from any work, thought or good deed on our own.

WB: In fact, this grace has been given to us as a gift, free of charge.

Some other suggestions you may want to incorporate in your explanation of Ephesians 2:8-9 include:

- A hypothetical scenario where you give the individual a gift on his or her birthday or at Christmas. In this example, you're trying to emphasize that the wrapped present given to the listener is free in the same way God gives us the gift of salvation (i.e. they don't have to earn or pay for it).

- To further clarify this passage, you could advise the listener that the only thing required to enjoy this, or any other gift is to simply receive it. In the same way, all that's required to experience the gift of salvation is to receive it through one's faith in Jesus Christ. Interestingly enough, this sets up the next verse in the plan of salvation.

> **Verse 4: Romans 10:13**
> "For whoever calls on the name of the Lord shall be saved."

WB: In the verse I just read (Romans 10:13) "calls on the name of the Lord" means to ask Jesus to be your Lord and Savior.

WB: Whoever does this will be saved or delivered from the penalty of sin, which is spiritual death—eternal separation from God.

WB: It doesn't say whosoever except _____ did it?
Fill in the blank with LP's name, your name, etc.

WB: No, it says whoever—meaning anyone—including you and I—who asks Jesus to be their Lord and Savior will be saved.

COACH'S TIP

Additional comments along with another verse will help you further clarify Romans 10:13 and Ephesians 2:8-9 if needed. They include:

WB: In the last few verses we looked at Romans 10:13 and Ephesians 2:8-9. Neither one of them stated that we have to keep the commandments, be good to our neighbor, go to church, or _____ did they?

- *LP responds by saying, "No."*
- *Fill in the blank above with one of the items from the Trust Statement stage (**Chapter 16**).*

WB: They only said one thing — by our faith in Jesus Christ.

WB: Another verse that helps to understand this more clearly is Romans 10:9, which states, *"If you confess with your mouth the Lord Jesus and believe in your heart that God has raised Him from the dead, you will be saved."*

LESSON WRAP UP

Great news, the course is almost over. Finally, right? With a laugh at my own expense. There are only two modules remaining: **Drawing the Net** and **Assurance of Salvation.** However, please don't brush these two aside as they're just as important as the other ones. You'll see why in a minute.

Before you move on to the next lesson (**Drawing the Net**) I hope you spend a few moments going over the Game Plan, Discussion Questions, and Personal Challenge sections at the end of this chapter. Each one will sharpen your witnessing skills as they provide some key tips and a role-play section for others within or outside your study group.

GAME PLAN

- ❑ Pray (ask) for the Holy Spirit's power to share the gospel.
- ❑ Review and memorize: Romans 3:23, 6:23; Revelations 20:14-15. Romans 5:8; 1 Corinthians 15:3-4; Ephesians 2:8-9; Romans 10:13.
- ❑ Highlight these verses in your Bible: Romans 3:23, 6:23; 10:13; 1 Corinthians 15:3-4; Ephesians 2:8-9, and Revelations 20:14-15.
- ❑ Role-play this lesson with two or more people. Take turns being the Witnessing Believer (WB) and the Lost Person (LP). See **Appendix A** in the back of the book for the role-playing script. *The idea is to practice outside of your comfort zone so you're ready and relaxed when a witnessing opportunity presents itself.*

DISCUSSION QUESTIONS

1. When sharing Romans 3:23 you can clarify "the glory of God" by comparing it to a target (i.e. none of us hit the mark). What is another example you could use?
2. Write out another scenario for explaining God's grace as its stated in Ephesians 2:8-9.
3. Can you think of another verse or verses to use in the bad news or good news phase of the plan of salvation? If so, what are they?
4. Discuss why people struggle with accepting God's grace?

PERSONAL CHALLENGE

This personal challenge involves two items.
1. Role-play Lessons 4 - 7 with someone else this week.
2. Memorize the bad and good news verses: Romans 3:23, 6:23, 10:13; 1 Corinthians 15:3-4; Ephesians 2:8-9; Revelations 20:14-15 *(feel free to paraphrase if you need to).*

CHAPTER 19

DRAWING THE NET

Lesson 9

Then He [Jesus] said to them, "Follow Me, and I will make you fishers of men."
Matthew 4:19

I love Matthew's account of Jesus recruiting His first disciples. The scene begins with Jesus walking along the Sea of Galilee and then stopping as He notices two men fishing. As the two brothers, Peter and Andrew, cast their net into the water Jesus makes a statement that would radically change their lives forever. He said, "Follow Me, and I will make you fishers of men" (Mt. 4:19).

As I think about the timing of Christ's statement, it couldn't have been more relevant. Especially when you consider that the primary tool of their trade was a net. They didn't have fiberglass fishing poles or artificial bait and tackle. That stuff didn't even exist at that time. Instead, anglers used large nets to catch fish. The bigger the net the more fish they could catch.

Consequently, the metaphor that Jesus uses is one that these men would clearly understand. Reason being, these brothers were fishermen. Fishing was their full-time occupation. It was how they made a living.

But casting their net into the water wasn't enough to reap the benefits of their catch. They had one more step to perform. In order to enjoy the fruit of their labor, they had to pull their net in. This same action applies today, regardless of the instrument you use to catch fish, albeit a net or a fishing pole.

When casting 'the net of the gospel' you and I still need to draw it in. How we do that is the focus of this chapter.

Up to this point in your presentation, you've laid out the whole roadmap of the gospel. The individual you've witnessed to has heard everything needed to surrender his or her life to Jesus Christ. Your job now is to guide the listener to a decision. Hopefully, one of commitment.

However, you can't assume that the individual you're speaking to fully comprehends the gospel message just because you shared the entire plan of salvation. Therefore, this stage of the gospel presentation is vital for two reasons. First, it helps to ensure the lost person fully understands the gospel. Second, this is the moment where you ask the individual the most important question of all: If they would like to trust Jesus Christ as their Lord and Savior.

> YOU CAN'T ASSUME THAT THE NON-BELIEVER FULLY COMPREHENDS THE GOSPEL MESSAGE JUST BECAUSE YOU SHARED THE ENTIRE PLAN OF SALVATION.

COACH'S TIP

If you've made it this far in your witnessing encounter this step is much easier than you think. For starters, the Holy Spirit is right there with you guiding your words. In addition, the Spirit of God is actively working in the heart of the non-believer. Finally, you've already built a sense of trust with the person you've been witnessing to as a result of the time they've given you.

KEEP IN MIND

Regardless of the outcome, there are several things you'll want to keep in mind. First and foremost, remember that their decision is not up to you. The choice that the individual makes is entirely up to them, through the power of the Holy Spirit. Next, if they're struggling with some aspect of the gospel, you'll be better equipped to give them an answer as a result of your training. Most importantly, if the potential believer is in full agreement, you will have just witnessed a miracle—their eternal salvation.

A GUIDE AND TEMPLATE

Listed below is a template that will guide you through this phase of the gospel presentation. Similar to previous sections, don't worry about repeating everything in the outline word for word. Instead, allow the Holy Spirit to be your guide and the information that follows as a blueprint to help you draw the net.

For your convenience, I've provided a couple of options that you can use in this step. If possible, practice each one a few times with someone else to determine which one you feel more comfortable with. You may find that different occasions require one method over the other. Regardless, the goal of each one is to summarize your gospel presentation in an effort to guide the individual to a decision.

DRAWING THE NET (OPTION 1)

WB: From our conversation, the Bible states that your eternal salvation is through your faith in Jesus Christ, nothing more and nothing less.

WB: To be sure you understand what we spoke about, I would like to ask you a few questions.

WB: Do you believe that you're a sinner and that your sin is bad enough to separate you from God?

LP: Yes.

WB: Do you believe that Jesus Christ is God and that He died on the cross for your sins?

LP: Yes.

WB: Now that you understand the gospel, would you like to ask Jesus to be your Lord and Savior?

LP: Yes

WB: That's great! I'm going to lead you in a simple prayer. Just so you know it's not a prayer that saves you, it's who you're trusting in—Jesus Christ—who does that.

WB: Let's pray.

WB: Please repeat after me.

WB: Dear Jesus.... I know that I'm a sinner... and that my sin deserves to be punished... But you loved me enough... to die on the cross, be buried, and rise again... I ask you to forgive me... for all my sins... I trust in you and you alone for my salvation... In Jesus name, Amen.

DRAWING THE NET (OPTION 2)

WB: So, LP, if you asked Jesus to save you what would He do?

LP: Save me.

WB: Exactly. Would He be saving you because you're good or because He's good?

LP: Because He's good.

WB: Would you be depending on what you do or what Jesus did to get you to heaven?

LP: What Jesus did.

WB: So, you realize you're a sinner and that your sin would cause you to come short of heaven and deserve to go to hell.
Note: This is where you can review key points of your conversation with the non-believer.

LP: Yes.

WB: And you believe that Jesus died for your sins and rose again.

LP: Yes.

WB: And now if you ask Him to save you what would He do?

LP: Save me.

> *Note: If the LP responds by saying they don't know, you can ask them what part (if any) they do not understand. Once they give you this information, I recommend going over that section again.*

WB: If I led you in a simple prayer, knowing that Jesus accepts you just as you are, would you be willing to let Him come into your heart and save you?

LP: Yes.

WB: Dear Jesus, help <u>LP</u> understand what we are about to say.

WB: <u>LP</u>, I simply want you to ask Jesus to save you.

WB: Let's Pray.

WB: Just repeat after me.

WB: Dear Jesus… I know that I'm a sinner… and that my sin deserves to be punished… I believe that you died for my sins… and rose again on the third day…. I trust in you and you alone for my salvation… I ask you to forgive me for all my sins… and be my Lord and Savior…. Right here and right now… In Jesus name, Amen.

> *Note:* *It's a good idea to pause between phrases of this prayer. This will allow the individual time to repeat what you have prayed.*

COACH'S TIP

We don't want to give an unsaved person the impression that a prayer gives them eternal life. Thus, you'll want to make sure they understand—before or after the prayer—that their profession of faith in Jesus Christ is what saves them. The Sinner's Prayer is simply a tool that helps a non-believer trust in Jesus.

LESSON WRAP-UP

When going through this phase of your presentation you may find that the non-believer is struggling with one or more aspects of the gospel. If so, take a few moments to go over those areas again using supportive verses where applicable. You can also have them read those verses out loud, if you haven't already.

Now that you've reviewed the lesson, let's go through the **Game Plan, Discussion Questions and Personal Challenge** section. You'll notice that I've listed the same prayer in this lesson as the previous one. The reason for this—as you may recall—is because you and I can only borrow the Holy Spirit's power to witness. Therefore, it's imperative that you ask for the Spirit's power to proclaim the good news.

For a **FREE handheld version** of this outline, turn to **Appendix C** of this book. That chapter introduces the **Pocket Gospel** which you can download for FREE. It can be downloaded at **JeffJerina.com/Books/FaithWithoutFear/PocketGospel.**

GAME PLAN

❑ Pray (ask) for the Holy Spirit's power to share the gospel.

❑ Read Matthew 4:18-22.

❑ Read and highlight John 5:24, Ephesians 1:13 and Hebrews 7:25 in your Bible.

❑ Role-play both of the **Drawing the Net** options with two or more people. Take turns being the Witnessing Believer (WB) and the Lost Person (LP). See **Appendix A** for the role-playing outline.

DISCUSSION QUESTIONS

1. Why do you think the disciples in Matthew 4:18-22 followed Jesus so quickly?

2. Learning from the four disciples' urgency to leave everything to follow Jesus in Matthew 4:18-22, what do you personally need to leave behind right now?

3. Which of the **Drawing the Net** options do you feel more comfortable with? Why?

4. Can you think of another way to draw the net of the gospel message? If so, discuss.

PERSONAL CHALLENGE

1. Memorize the three verses I had you highlight in the **Game Plan** section. These verses are instrumental in helping the new believer understand their salvation is secure.

2. Role-play all eight lessons of the gospel presentation as one unit with someone else this week.

CHAPTER 20

ASSURANCE OF SALVATION

Lesson 10

*In Him you also trusted, after you heard the word of
truth, the gospel of your salvation; in whom also, having
believed, you were sealed with the Holy Spirit of
promise...*
Ephesians 1:13

This is the last stage in the gospel presentation. It's the point where you assure the new believer that their salvation is secure, based on their profession of faith in Jesus. In addition, this step will reaffirm key points you made throughout your conversation. Likewise, you'll have the opportunity to introduce some important truths that will help the new Christian even more. With that said, here's a brief summary of the items you'll want to convey:

- Assure the individual that their salvation is secure.
- Verify that the new believer understands that Jesus is the one who saved them.
- Remind them that Jesus saved them because He's good and not because their good.
- Encourage the individual to tell others about the good news

of their salvation. Every time they do this, they will be sharing their personal testimony.

- Make sure the person understands that they don't have to repeatedly ask Jesus to be their Lord and Savior. Similar to being born physically, spiritual birth in Jesus Christ happens only once (see John 3:3; 1 Pet. 1:23).

NOTE:

It's been my experience that the last item (listed above) is frequently missed when assuring the new believer of their salvation. I mention this because I continually meet people who believe they have to ask Jesus to be their Lord and Savior every time they hear an altar call or as a means of penance when they sin. Thus, it's a good idea to remind the individual that their profession of faith in Jesus—that they made at the moment of their salvation—gives them eternal life, once and for all (see John 3:16, 5:24, 10:28; Rom. 8:38-39, 10:13; 1 John 5:12-13).

COACH'S TIP

In addition to the points above, you can:

- Obtain their contact information to follow-up at a later time.
- Ask if they have a Bible. If not, you can give them a small handheld one or encourage them to purchase a digital study Bible we have available at **MenUnplugged.net/Bible** (this will ensure they can access God's Word on any device).
- Ask the new believer to visit your home group or church.
- Encourage the individual to listen to the *Men Unplugged* show. It will encourage and equip them in their daily walk.

Listed in the following outline is a template to guide you in communicating this truth to a new Christian. Please note in this section that 'LP' has been changed to 'NC' as the former non-believer is now a new disciple of Jesus Christ.

ASSURANCE OF SALVATION (OUTLINE)

WB: Congratulations <u>NC</u>! You have just made the most important decision you'll ever make. By your profession of faith in Jesus Christ the Bible states that you have eternal life.

Note: Read out loud or have the new believer read out loud John 5:24.

WB: The Bible states that your salvation is complete.

WB: Hebrews 7:25 tells us that Jesus Christ has saved you to the "uttermost". This word 'uttermost' means complete in every sense of the word. It means that there is nothing else that you have to do for your salvation.

WB: Who did you ask to save you?

NC: Jesus.

WB: Did Jesus save you because you're good or because He's good?

NC: Because He's good.

WB: Did He save you for a little while or forever?

NC: Forever.

WB: Absolutely.

COACH'S TIP

Another verse you can share with the new Christian is Ephesians 1:13. It states, "In Him [Jesus Christ] you also trusted, after you heard the word of truth, the gospel of your salvation; in whom also, having believed, you were sealed with the Holy Spirit of promise."

If you prefer using this verse (which I often do), I would suggest saying something like this:

WB: This seal is not something that you and I can break like a seal on a package. On the contrary, because it's of eternal origin

(God sealed it) there's nothing that can break it. That's good news for all of us, since we are still going to mess up or sin.

LESSON WRAP-UP

Hallelujah! Glory to God! If you've made it to this point in your presentation of the gospel you've just witnessed a miracle. The individual who responded to the gospel message is now a new creation in Christ Jesus (see 2 Cor. 5:17). They've passed from spiritual death to eternal life (see John 5:24).

Because of your preparation and willingness to proclaim the gospel, the individual was able to hear the good news. Thereby, prompting them—through the power of the Holy Spirit—to make a faith-based decision to trust Jesus Christ as their personal savior. This is something that Paul made clear to the believers in Rome when he encouraged them to preach the gospel to the Jews.

Paul's exhortation to the church of Rome can be summarized in two verses, Romans 10:14 and Romans 10:17. When paraphrasing his charge, we learn that "faith comes by hearing…the word of God" shared through professing believers (Rom. 10:17). What an excellent reminder from our Christian brother to do our part in evangelism.

For a **FREE handheld version** of this outline, turn to **Appendix C** of this book. That chapter introduces the **Pocket Gospel** which you can download for FREE. It can be downloaded at **JeffJerina.com/Books/FaithWithoutFear/PocketGospel**.

GAME PLAN

❑ Pray (ask) for the courage to proactively share the gospel.

❑ Read Romans 10:14-17.

❑ Role-play this section with one or more individuals. Take turns being the Witnessing Believer (WB) and the New Christian (NC). See **Appendix A** for more help.

❑ Role-play all nine phases of the gospel presentation with one or more individuals. Practice taking turns being the Witnessing Believer (WB) and the Lost Person (LP) / New Christian (NC). If you need a comprehensive outline, please see the one listed in **Appendix A** of this book.

❑ Download your **FREE** copy of the **Pocket Gospel** in **Appendix C** and place it in your Bible, wallet or purse.

DISCUSSION QUESTIONS

1. In Romans 10:14 the word 'preacher' is the same word used in Mark 16:15, the Greek word 'kerysso'. It means to proclaim, teach, tell, or share. Now that you know the meaning of the word 'preacher' in these verses, does it change the way you think of your role as a disciple of Christ? Explain.

2. Can you think of other verses that will help assure the new believer of their eternal salvation? Discuss.

3. Do you think this part in the gospel presentation is hard for Christians to execute? If so, why?

4. What fears (if any) do you have now about witnessing?

PERSONAL CHALLENGE

1. Share the gospel to someone this week. This can be a friend, family member, neighbor, co-worker, or someone you just met.

2. Review the **Dealing with Objections** section in the next chapter.

CHAPTER 21

DEALING WITH
OBJECTIONS

Lesson 11

*Walk in wisdom toward those who are outside, redeeming
the time. Let your speech always be with grace, seasoned
with salt, that you may know how you ought to answer
each one.*
Colossians 4:5-6

T his chapter highlights two objections a non-believer may have
towards the gospel. The intent here is not to describe each one
in full detail, but rather to give you an idea of how to respond in each
situation.

Although the responses will help you defend your faith, please
know that they will never replace the work of the Holy Spirit in a lost
person's heart. Moreover, they are not a substitute for the words that
God will give you in each witnessing encounter.

In short, as I mentioned in a previous chapter: You can't defend
your faith unless you first know how to share it. With this in mind,
there are four things you'll want to remember when responding to
objections.

1. **Make sure that you respond with love, confidence and self-control.** "For God has not given us a spirit of fear, but of power and of love and of a sound mind. Therefore, do not be ashamed of the testimony of our Lord..." (2 Tim. 1:7-8a).

2. **Don't let objections deter or force you off track.** Our enemy, the devil, doesn't want the good news to be shared. For he knows that "the gospel of Christ... is the power of God to salvation for all those who believe" (Rom. 1:16).

3. **Let God sell Himself through His goodness and His Word.** Remember, neither you nor I can win someone to Christ. It's only through the power of the Holy Spirit that a person is saved. Thus, the more Scripture that you bring into your answers, the more effective your responses will be.

   a. Romans 2:4 states, "The goodness of God leads people to repentance."
   b. Hebrews 4:12 states, "For the word of God is living and powerful, and sharper than any two-edged sword, piercing even to the division of soul and spirit, and of joints and marrow, and is a discerner of the thoughts and intents of the heart."

4. **When using analogies or examples, make sure they're relevant to the individual's questions.** Keep in mind that the stories you share don't have to be some elaborate illustration. Nor do they need to contain a complex theological argument. They just need to be ones that are simple to understand by the individual you're sharing the gospel with.

Listed below are a few objections you may run across and how you can deal with them if they do.

OBJECTION #1

This objection is a general dissent by the non-believer or opportunity by the devil to thwart the gospel from being shared. The interruption may occur at any point during your presentation of the gospel. When you run across this—in your evangelistic efforts—consider using the following technique. The idea behind this response is to prevent you from going down endless rabbit trails in search for an answer. As a result, you're giving the listener an opportunity to hear and respond to the gospel message itself; thereby, allowing the Holy Spirit to work in the heart of that person.

LP: But what about this.
Or the individual you're speaking to may say something along the lines of, "That contradicts what this verse says", or "That's different than I've heard before."

WB: I often wondered that myself. Then I heard what I'm going to share with you, and it answered my questions.

WB: It may do the same for you.

WB: If you wouldn't mind, I'd like to finish what I was sharing.
Or you could say, "If I could finish what I was saying. It may answer your questions."

COACH'S TIP

If your response is unsuccessful in allowing you to continue the gospel presentation, consider giving the lost person a gospel tract, a New Testament Bible, or pointing them to a website that shares the plan of salvation (i.e. **MenUnplugged.net/Gospel**). Most of the time, the individual will read one of those items at a later date.

OBJECTION #2

This rebuttal is given from someone with a 'works-based' mentality. The individual who responds this way thinks their good deeds have to outweigh their bad actions in order to spend eternity in heaven. When you're dealing with this type of objection, you'll want to share a personal or biblical story that clearly illustrates God's grace is all that's needed for salvation. Listed below is an example of what your conversation may look like in a real-life witnessing encounter.

NOTE:

Quite often, the individual will know who Jesus is and many times believe in Jesus Christ already. However, they're not *trusting* in Him for their salvation. The distinguishing factor in their viewpoint is that they believe you have to do something (i.e. good works) to be saved. Whereas, the Bible is clear that it's based on the work that Christ has already completed at Calvary (see Acts 16:31; John 3:16; Rom. 10:9; Eph. 2:8-9). This is important to understand when you're speaking with someone because what they're really saying is that they *believe* that Jesus exists but don't *trust* in Him for their salvation.

LP: Yes, but we still have to do good things to go to heaven.

WB: You're right. God does want us to do good things.

WB: However, that's not a requirement for salvation or going to heaven when we die.

WB: You remember earlier when I shared with you that it's by grace that we've been saved through faith.

WB: Do you know that grace is undeserved favor?

WB: By this I mean that all of the bad things that you and I have ever done or will do in our lives deserve the ultimate punishment— eternal separation from God.

WB: However, God took all of our sins upon Himself when the second person of the Triune Godhead, Jesus Christ, stepped away from the other two persons of the Trinity to come to earth in human form, to die on the cross for your sins and mine.

WB: In short, it's a free gift that God has given us through our faith in Jesus Christ.

WB: Just like you receive a birthday present or a gift from someone, you don't have to do anything for that gift.

ALTERNATE RESPONSE TO OBJECTION #2

WB: Remember the story of Jesus on the cross.

WB: To be on that cross—with the exception of Jesus—you had to live in such a way that you continually broke the law. In fact, this form of punishment was the worst they had back then. If you remember from the story, there were also two thieves on crosses. One of them turned to Jesus and said, "Remember me when you enter your kingdom" (Luke 23:42). Jesus answered, consider it done (see Luke 23:41-43). Now think about this. *There is no way that thief could have taken the straps from his wrists and feet and then climbed down 10 or so feet from the cross to perform his one good deed.* Not to mention, put himself back up on the cross—with little to no energy or strength left—now could he? Obviously not. All he did was ask Jesus to save him. And Jesus did. If Jesus gave this man (an individual who lived a life of habitual sin) eternal life, don't you think he would do the same for you?

LP: Absolutely!

COACH'S TIP

Remind the non-believer that the good things that God wants us to do are because of the love He has for us, not because these things earn our way to salvation. A good supporting verse here is Ephesians 2:8-9, as it specifically states that it's by grace (not works) that we are saved. Another passage to bring in for this response is Romans 4:1-25, more specifically verses 3, 13, 16, and 24-25. In this passage Paul reminds believers that Abraham was justified by faith alone, not by works. These verses can also help when responding to those of the Jewish or Muslim faith.

LESSON WRAP-UP

I have great news for you. This was the final training module. Which means you have officially completed your evangelism training. If you weren't already, you're now equipped to provide an accurate presentation of the gospel through the power of the Holy Spirit.

Regardless of the objections you receive, the most important thing to remember is that every time you share the gospel, you're giving the listener an opportunity to hear and respond to God's free gift of salvation. If you can, take a few days to complete the following **Game Plan, Discussion Questions,** and **Personal Challenge** unit to sharpen your witnessing skills.

Before you go, I want to encourage you to read the remaining sections of this book. You'll find encouraging words, key resources, as well as, links to other valuable resources to strengthen your walk and unleash your witnessing efforts even more. More specifically:

- In the **Conclusion**, you'll be inspired to share your faith as I highlight a few well-known and unexpected biblical figures that God used to proclaim His name.

- **Appendix A** contains the complete role-playing outline for the gospel presentation you learned in Lessons 4 through 10.

- **Appendix B** lists the Scripture verses outlined in Lessons 4 through 10 of this book.

- **Appendix C** introduces *The Pocket Gospel*: An invaluable resource that contains the abridged version of the plan of salvation method learned in this book.

- **Appendix D** is a poem that shares the gospel presentation.

- In the chapter titled, **Sharing the Truth**, you'll find another method for sharing the gospel. You can use it right away to share your faith with confidence and power.

- The **Would You Like More Help** section provides links to additional resources and courses that will help you in your Christian walk and witnessing journey.

- **Creating a Culture of Evangelism** is for those in full-time or bi-vocational ministry. It helps leaders create and maintain a culture of evangelism within their church or ministry.

- **About the Author** and **Contact Jeff** sections provide more information about this author; how to get a hold of me for speaking engagements, training, coaching, and how to listen to and support **Men Unplugged**.

Visit **JeffJerina.com** for additional resources.

GAME PLAN

❑ Pray (ask) for the ability to respond with love and kindness to the objections you may receive.

❑ Role-play the objections in this lesson with two or more people. Take turns being the Witnessing Believer (WB) and the Lost Person (LP). See **Appendix A** for more help.

❑ Share the gospel to a non-believer this week. This can be a friend, family member, neighbor, co-worker, or someone you just met.

DISCUSSION QUESTIONS

1. What are some other objections that you've heard when sharing the gospel?

2. Discuss another response to Objection #1 that allows the believer to hear the gospel message.

3. What are some other verses or biblical accounts that can help you overcome these or other objections?

PERSONAL CHALLENGE

1. Role-play the first 10 lessons of the training again with another person this week. Take turns being the Witnessing Believer and the Lost Person/New Christian. If you need a comprehensive outline, please see the one provided in **Appendix A**.

2. If you haven't done so already, check out the resources available on my personal website **JeffJerina.com**, including:

   o An add-on course at **JeffJerina.com/Courses**.
   o The *Men Unplugged* show, which includes testimonies of top Christian leaders and tips on how to share the gospel. To subscribe and listen for free go to **MenUnplugged.net**.

CONCLUSION

T hank you again for your time and dedication to fulfill the Great Commission. Your faithful proclamation of the gospel is vital in expanding the kingdom of God. Regardless of your age, spiritual maturity, ethnicity, occupation, marital status or gender, the Creator of the universe wants to use you to reach the lost. As a matter of fact, there is biblical record of the Lord using people from all walks of life to proclaim His name.

Can you recall who the first evangelists were in the New Testament? Quite honestly, I use to think it was the early disciples until I read the Christmas story to my daughter one year. In the second chapter of Luke, we read the account of the angels appearing before the shepherds (Luke 2:8-20). What's interesting about this story is that the Lord sent His angels to this ordinary group of people to announce the birth of Christ. In other words, some of the most uneducated, unclean, and unlikeliest individuals were given the initial task of proclaiming the good news of Jesus Christ.

How about the Samaritan woman at the well? Detailed in John's account, we learn that she shared her testimony of how Jesus knew everything about her. As a result of her personal witness, many people in that region placed their faith in Jesus Christ (see John 4:39). What's even more amazing is that she did this without any formal or informal evangelism training. Further proof that the hard part of conversion is performed by the Holy Spirit.

Consider the first disciples. At least a third of them—as we discussed in previous chapters—were fishermen. Which meant that the majority—if not all—were uneducated and financially burdened. However, Jesus chose them to radically transform the world. He used this band of 11 (I'm excluding Judas Iscariot) to reach the lost and equip the saved with His gospel message. Their contributions to Christendom and the spread of the gospel cannot be underscored.

Lastly, I want to mention one of my favorites and possibly yours too, the apostle Paul. Here's a man that despised, hated, and killed Christians. But through God's amazing grace, Paul was miraculously transformed by his encounter with Jesus Christ (see Acts 9:1-19). The apostle's conversion may have been the quickest and most radical turnarounds in all of history. To go from an individual who hated everything that Christians stood for, to arguably the greatest Christian evangelist of all time can only be described as supernatural.

My hope in sharing these biblical examples is to encourage you in your own personal witnessing efforts. Furthermore, I hope you're reminded that our part in evangelism is to *always be ready* to share the gospel. God's part in evangelism—through the power of the Holy Spirit—is to 1) empower the believer to witness and 2) to win others to Christ. If you can remember this, you'll be able to boldly preach the good news of Jesus Christ to anyone you come across. At any time. Anywhere.

Additionally, your faithfulness will—more than likely—become a catalyst for other believers to fulfill the gospel mandate as well. This is something that the apostle Paul observed during his Roman imprisonment. You can read about that story in Philippians 1:12-18.

In short, I hope that you'll leave this training better equipped and more passionate about God's command to reach the lost. Moreover, I hope that this book will help spread the gospel message across the globe. Ultimately, I pray that this training in some way will be used by you and other Christians to help unsaved individuals experience the greatest victory of all—freedom in Jesus Christ.

Visit JeffJerina.com for additional training, courses, workshops, my speaking topics, books, and other resources that are designed to help you ignite your faith and succeed in life.

Appendix A

GOSPEL PRESENTATION

Full Outline

WB = Witnessing Believer
LP = Lost Person
NC = New Christian

SHARING YOUR TESTIMONY (LESSON 5)

WB: Someone once asked me if I knew that I would go to heaven when I die or if I would have doubts? I wasn't really sure. They shared something with me that helped me understand without a shadow of doubt that I would go to Heaven! Let me ask you the same thing. If you were to die today, would you be 100% sure that you would go to heaven or would you have doubts like I did? *(Wait for LP's response)*

THE TRUST STATEMENT (LESSON 6)

WB: In your opinion, what do you think you would have to do to in order to go to heaven?

Note: Please remember that you're trying to find out what the individual believes is required for salvation. To help them understand your question, you can clarify it with the other questions below. You don't have to ask these other questions, but you may feel like you need to in order to better clarify their answers. As you may recall, asking questions is a great way to understand where the individual is now, spiritually. After each question, you'll want to wait for their response.

How about believing in God?
How about doing good things?
How about keeping the commandments?
How about being kind to your neighbor?
How about getting baptized?

WB: So basically, you're depending on several things to get you to heaven.

WB: Is that correct?

SHARING THE GOSPEL (LESSON 7)

WB: Romans 1:16 states, "the gospel is the power of God to salvation for everyone who believes…"

WB: The word 'gospel' means **good news**.

WB: When we translate the gospel into the original language that it was written in, Greek, the actual definition is 'good news'.

WB: But in order to appreciate the good news we have to understand the bad news first.

WB: The bad news is something about all of us.

SHARING THE BAD AND GOOD NEWS (LESSON 8)

THE BAD NEWS

WB: Romans 3:23 says that "All have sinned and fall short of the glory of God."

WB: All of us have done or thought something wrong at one point in our lives.

WB: Even a lie that you tell your parents when you were a kid to keep you from getting in trouble is wrong.

WB: I've told a few lies before.

WB: How about you?

LP: Yes.

WB: In the Bible, this wrong action—even a tiny lie is called sin. Because of our sin we have to realize that we miss God's mark of perfection, or as the Bible states—the glory of God. Which means that we are all sinners.

WB: But the bad news gets worse.

WB: Romans 6:23 says "The wages of sin is death, but the gift of God is eternal life in Christ Jesus our Lord."

WB: The wages or payment for just one sin the Bible says is death.

WB: Not just physical but spiritual death.

WB: As such, the Bible states that a soul must face a spiritual death or what the Bible calls the second death.

WB: Revelation 20:14-15 tells us "… The lake of fire is the second death. Anyone whose name was not found written in the book of life was thrown into the lake of fire." *(Rev. 20:14-15 NIV)*

WB: Just as the bad news got worse the good news gets even better.

THE GOOD NEWS

WB: Romans 5:8 says that "God demonstrates His own love toward us, in that while we were still sinners, Christ died for us."

WB: What this verse is telling us is that God meets you and I where we are right now. Regardless of whatever good or bad we may have done in our lives.

WB: He gives us the ultimate solution to our problem of sin through the work of Jesus Christ. Let me explain.

WB: 1 Corinthians 15:3-4 states that Jesus died for our sins, He was buried, and He rose again on the third day.

WB: His sacrifice on the cross paid for all of your sins—past, present and future.

WB: Ephesians 2:8-9 says, "by grace you have been saved, through faith—and this is not from yourselves, it is the gift of God—not of works, so that no one can boast." *(Eph. 2:8-9 NIV)*

WB: Did you know that the word 'grace' means undeserved favor?

WB: In other words, you and I were given something we don't deserve—a full pardon for our sins.

WB: What's even better is that you and I were given this apart from any work, thought or good deed on our own.

WB: This grace has been given to us as a gift—free of charge.

WB: Meaning we can't earn it by anything we do or don't do.

DRAWING THE NET (LESSON 9)

WB: From our conversation, the Bible states that your eternal salvation is through your faith in Jesus Christ, nothing more and nothing less.

WB: To be sure that you understand what I've shared, I would like to ask you a few questions.

WB: Do you believe that you're a sinner?

LP: Yes.

WB: Do you believe your sin is bad enough to separate you from God?

WB: Do you believe that Jesus Christ is God and that He died on the cross for your sins and rose from the grave?

LP: Yes.

WB: Now that you understand the gospel, would you like to ask Jesus to save you?

LP: Yes.

WB: Just so you'll know it's not a prayer that saves you, it's who you're trusting in—Jesus Christ who does that.

WB: Let's pray.

SINNER'S PRAYER

WB: Repeat after me.

WB: Dear Jesus.... I know that I am a sinner... and that my sin causes me to be separated from you... But you loved me enough... to die on the cross, be buried, and rise again... I ask you to forgive me... for all my sins... I trust in you and you alone for my salvation... In Jesus name, Amen.

ASSURANCE OF SALVATION (LESSON 10)

WB: Congratulations <u>NC</u>! You have just made the most important decision you will ever make.

WB: By your profession of faith in Jesus Christ, the Bible states that you have eternal life.

Read out loud or have the new believer read out loud John 5:24.

WB: The Bible states that your salvation is complete.

WB: Hebrews 7:25 tells us that Jesus has saved you to the uttermost.

WB: That word 'uttermost' means complete in every sense of the word.

WB: Meaning that there is nothing else that needs to be done for your salvation.

WB: Who did you call upon?

NC: Jesus.

WB: What did you ask Him to do?

NC: Save me.

WB: Did Jesus save you because you're good or because He's good?

NC: Because He's good.

WB: Did He save you for a little while or forever?

NC: Forever.

WB: So, if you died 10 minutes from now where would you go?

NC: Heaven.

WB: How about _____ years from now?

Fill in the blank with whatever number you want, 10, 20, 30, 40, etc.

NC: Heaven.

WB: Do you think so or know so?

NC: I know so.

SCRIPTURE OUTLINE

Share Your Testimony

The Trust Statement

Share the Gospel

- Romans 1:16
- 1 Corinthians 15:1-4

  Can be used in the good news section below.

Share the Bad and Good News

The Bad News:

- Romans 3:23 *(Romans 3:10 can be added to this section).*
- Romans 6:23
- Revelation 20:14-15

The Good news:

- Romans 5:8
- 1 Corinthians 15:1-4

  If already shared, you don't need to share this verse again.

- Romans 10:13
- Ephesians 2:8-9

Draw the Net

- Romans 10:9 *(Titus 1:2 can be added in this step).*

Assurance of Salvation

- John 5:24; Hebrews 7:25; or Ephesians 1:13

THE POCKET GOSPEL

The pocket gospel is an excellent tool in assisting new soul-winners, as well as, seasoned evangelists in presenting the plan of salvation. It's especially useful for those moments when a witnessing believer has trouble remembering a particular Scripture verse or spiritual question to ask a non-believer. I would suggest making several laminated copies of it and placing one in your daily Bible, another in your wallet or purse, and an additional one in your vehicle.

GET YOUR FREE COPY

As a thank you for your purchase of this book, I would like to offer you a FREE digital copy of the Pocket Gospel. You can download your FREE copy at:

https://JeffJerina.com/Books/FaithWithoutFear/PocketGospel

Appendix D

A PRODIGAL'S JOURNEY

The following poem reflects my personal journey to find Jesus Christ. Although it communicates my testimony, I've written it in such a way that anyone can relate to it. I hope it blesses and encourages you.

You can purchase a digital / print copy of the poem for personal or corporate use at **JeffJerina.com/Store**. While there, you'll notice that I've overlaid the poem (same content) over two different pictures. Those versions are great as inspirational wall art or as a gift to someone else you know.

GET YOUR DIGITAL COPY

Get your copy of *A Prodigal's Journey* (available in various sizes) at:

https://JeffJerina.com/Store

A Prodigal's Journey

Woe is me said the prodigal son.
I have tried it all, yes for fun.
My sins and bad choices I do regret.
They have caused me pain and so much fret.
As I stumbled and fell in this life for years,
all this world had for me I thought was tears.

Lost and broken with no hope in sight,
I heard God's voice—who shined The Light.
He said I love you and always will,
despite your sins or how bad you feel.
My beloved Son died for you and the world years ago.
This one thing is all you need to know.

The King of kings touched my soul deep within.
He said trust in Me, and your life will begin.
Not for a day, a month, or even a year,
But for all eternity so have no fear.
I said it seems too simple, don't I have to pay.
And then He whispered to me that

He is the Way.

With joy I shouted at the top of my voice,
Jesus Christ, my Lord and Savior, in you I made my choice!
From eternity past to now and beyond,
Christ is my ransom and everlasting bond.
Because of Christ's sacrifice I have been given new life.
One with everlasting joy, peace, and no more strife.

Now GO out into the world and tell all of mankind.
That Jesus Christ alone saves and to each He can find.
So, as I live my life seeking those who are lost,
Christ said, tell everyone that Yes, they're worth the cost.
If they doubt the Gospel is real,
I will tell them how amazing God's grace makes me feel.

— Jeff Jerina © 2015

SHARING THE TRUTH

Another Way to Share the Gospel

This chapter contains an alternative method I often use to share the gospel. Just like the approach we've covered already; this template is simple to learn and share as well.

Right away, you'll notice that the role-playing features and follow-up sections are removed to kickstart your witnessing efforts. In addition, I've intentionally excluded the *Personal Testimony* and *Trust Statement* steps, as we learned about those in previous chapters. Therefore, the following outline is a continuation from your personal testimony being shared, and the individual acknowledging their *Trust Statement*. In this case, the person you're speaking to is unsure of their salvation.

Here are four truths you'll want to communicate and how to go about sharing each one.

TRUTH #1: GOD LOVES THEM

THE FIRST TRUTH YOU'LL WANT TO SHARE IS THAT GOD LOVES THEM.

You can say something like this:
In your joy and pain, through your good and bad, no matter what… God loves and cares for you.

You can then recite John 3:16:

For a **FREE handheld version** of this method, go to **Appendix C** of this book.

> "For God so loved the world that He gave His one and only Son, that whoever believes in Him shall not perish, but have eternal life."

TRUTH #2: THERE'S SOME BAD NEWS

THE SECOND TRUTH THAT YOU'LL WANT TO CONVEY IS THAT THERE'S 'SOME BAD NEWS' AND THIS 'BAD NEWS' IS TRUE FOR EVERYONE.

You can say:

The 'bad news' separates us from God, whether it's something we've said, thought, or done. The Bible calls these bad things 'sin'.

You can then recite Romans 3:23:

> "For all have sinned and fall short of the glory of God."

Then say:

But the bad news gets worse. Because just one bad thing we say or do causes us to be separated from God.

You can recite the first part of Romans 6:23:

> "For the wages of sin is death [i.e. spiritual death] …"

NEXT, YOU'LL WANT TO MAKE A TRANSITION STATEMENT FROM THE BAD NEWS OF MAN'S SIN PROBLEM TO THE GOOD NEWS OF THE GOSPEL (CHRIST'S SOLUTION TO OUR PROBLEM OF SIN).

You can say something like:

This bad news doesn't have to last. God gave us the ultimate solution to our problem of sin. He gave us the gospel, which is the good news of Jesus Christ!

TRUTH #3: THE GOOD NEWS

THE THIRD TRUTH YOU'LL WANT TO SHARE IS THE GOOD NEWS, THE GOSPEL OF JESUS CHRIST.

You can do this by letting the individual know that:
God sent His Son, Jesus Christ, to die for our sins. In other words, Christ did something that you and I cannot do on our own—He paid the penalty for all of our sins (past, present, and future). He suffered on a cross so that you and I could have a personal relationship with Him forever.

Then you can recite Romans 5:8:

> "God demonstrates his own love for us in this: While we were still sinners, Christ died for us."

TO HELP THE NON-BELIEVER UNDERSTAND WHAT THE GOSPEL IS AND HOW THAT FREES THEM FROM THE PENALTY OF SIN (SPIRITUAL DEATH OR ETERNAL SEPARATION OF GOD).

You can say something like this:
Jesus gave up His life so you could be free from the penalty of sin! Not just for one day or one year, but for all eternity!

Then you can recite Romans 8:1-2:

> "Therefore, there is now no condemnation for those who are in Christ Jesus, because through Christ Jesus the law of the Spirit who gives life has set you free from the law of sin and death."

NEXT, YOU'LL WANT THE INDIVIDUAL TO KNOW THAT THE GOOD NEWS GETS EVEN BETTER.

You can do so by saying:

The good news gets better… Jesus rose again and is still alive today.

Then you can paraphrase 1 Corinthians 15:3-4:

> Jesus Christ died for our sins, was buried, and on the third day rose again.

TRUTH #4: SALVATION IS FREE

THE FOURTH TRUTH THAT YOU'LL WANT TO SHARE IS THAT GOD'S GIFT OF SALVATION IS FREE AND THAT ALL THEY HAVE TO DO TO RECEIVE IT IS TRUST IN JESUS CHRIST AS THEIR LORD AND SAVIOR.

You can do this by helping them understand that they cannot earn their way to heaven by doing good deeds or works. In other words, it's important that the person comprehends that Jesus has already paid for their sins (once and for all). All they have to do is trust in the work He completed 2000 years ago.

You can say something similar to:
You can be sure that your salvation is secure by simply trusting in the work that Jesus Christ did on the cross for you 2000 years ago. You cannot earn your way to heaven. It's a free gift, by grace (which is underserved favor) through your faith in Jesus Christ.

You can then recite Ephesians 2:8-9:

> "For by grace you have been saved through faith, and that not of yourselves; it is the gift of God, not of works…"

ONCE YOU HAVE SHARED THESE 4 TRUTHS, YOU CAN INVITE THEM TO RECEIVE JESUS CHRIST AS THEIR LORD AND SAVIOR.

You can do this by saying:

God is waiting for you. He does not exclude anyone from eternal life!

You can then recite Romans 10:13:

"Whoever calls on the name of the Lord [Jesus Christ] will be saved."

Then recite Romans 10:9:

The Bible says, "if you confess with your mouth that Jesus is Lord and believe in your heart that God raised him from the dead, you will be saved [delivered from spiritual death]."

ASK THE INDIVIDUAL IF HE OR SHE WOULD LIKE TO TRUST JESUS CHRIST AS THEIR LORD AND SAVIOR.

Make sure they understand that they are placing their faith in Jesus Christ, knowing that it's because of what He did for them (that He died, was buried and rose again on the third day) and because of that, they can have eternal life as they trust in Him and Him alone.

Alternatively, you can ask them if they would like to receive God's free gift of salvation?

IF THEY SAY YES, YOU CAN LEAD THEM IN A PRAYER LIKE THIS:

Dear Jesus, I know that I'm a sinner and that my sin deserves to be punished. But you loved me enough to die on a cross, be buried, and rise again. I trust in you and you alone for my salvation. I ask you to forgive me for all my sins and be my Lord and Savior. In Jesus name, Amen.

Please note: The prayer above (as we already discussed in **Chapter 19**) does not save a person. An individual's trust in Jesus Christ for their salvation, believing they have salvation because of what He did for them as opposed to their own good deeds, is what saves a person. However, this prayer (often called the Sinner's Prayer) is a good tool to employ as it reaffirms the commitment they just made.

IF THE PERSON REPLIES "NO" TO THE QUESTION ABOVE, YOU CAN RESPOND WITH ONE OF THE WAYS LISTED IN TABLE 1 OF **CHAPTER 16**.

For a **FREE handheld version** of this method, visit **JeffJerina.com/Books/FaithWithoutFear/PocketGospel** to download your FREE digital copy. Requires a photocopy or screenshot of your proof of purchase of this book.

WOULD YOU LIKE MORE HELP?

If you need more help, I have several options for you to consider. These resources can be used for individual or group training.

1. **My online evangelism training course.** This additional, self-paced course provides an overview of this book along with some useful tips, advice and role-playing sessions that I've found beneficial when witnessing. For more information or to register online visit the courses page at: **JeffJerina.com.**

2. **Formal group training.** This training is great for churches, mission teams, ministries, Christian schools, retreats and conventions. This is a highly interactive coaching session that will help jumpstart your outreach efforts. The course typically runs six to eight hours. However, I've customized the training to meet multiple time constraints. The tailored format can be either two to four hours in length. Additional training can be provided to help create and maintain a culture of evangelism in your ministry, school, or church. Feel free to contact me to discuss an option that will best fit your group. **jeff@MenUnplugged.net**

3. **Keynote speeches.** This option is great if you're looking to jumpstart or maintain a culture of evangelism in your church, ministry, or school. It's also beneficial if you prefer an abridged version of the training. To find out more about these and other presentations I offer simply contact me via email at

jeff@MenUnplugged.net. My contact information can also be found at the back of this book (chapter titled **Contact Jeff**).

4. **Men Unplugged show.** Every week I chat with top Christian leaders on key topics to help men—of any age and stage of life—and their families:

   √ Ignite their faith in Christ
   √ Strengthen their family
   √ Live with power and purpose
   √ Provide practical tips and solutions to succeed in life

   Visit **MenUnplugged.net/Podcast** to hear each episode.

As you listen to the show, you'll be encouraged and equipped as each guest shares their personal testimony, life lessons and words of wisdom to help you live out God's call on your life. In addition, you'll gain tips on how to share and defend your faith.

You'll hear from top Christian leaders like Josh McDowell, Dr. Gary Chapman, JC Watts, Dennis Rainey, Gary Thomas, Steve Arterburn, Dr. David Cook, Sean McDowell, musicians, actors, professional athletes, business and military leaders, and more.

5. **Additional Resources:** In addition to the *Men Unplugged* talk show, we have a collection of resources to deepen your walk with the Lord, strengthen your family, and stay equipped as a disciple of Christ. To access all of these resources go to: **MenUnplugged.net/Resources.**

I look forward to hearing from you,

Jeff

CREATING A CULTURE OF EVANGELISM

A Word to those in Ministry

Does your church lack a culture of evangelism? Are you struggling to engage your congregation in fulfilling the Great Commission?

If your answer to one or both of these questions is "Yes", I hope you'll consider a possible solution. Something that's easier to obtain than you think.

The remedy isn't in a sermon that you or one of your peers preach behind a pulpit. It's not even in the numerous ministries that are created to fulfill a need within and surrounding your community. As great as these are, neither of them can preserve a soul-winning lifestyle.

So, what can? Hoping to find an answer to this question, I began visiting other churches and asking other pastors about their specific game plan for evangelism. What I learned was quite telling.

Most of the churches I visited lacked the necessary strategy to cultivate evangelism. Without any fault of their own, those in leadership missed the most important aspect. This component, when executed consistently, will motivate your church body to consistently share the gospel.

Okay what is it? The answer is leadership. I'm not talking about a particular skill set or spiritual gifting that you or someone else needs to have. I'm referring to the kind of leadership that provides a model for others to follow.

When training His band of twelve, Jesus provided the ideal model for evangelism. He didn't just command these first disciples to proclaim the gospel, He was active in this ministry as well (see John 20:21). In short, this was His ultimate mission (see Luke 19:10). As a result, their zeal for preaching the good news never wavered as they watched the Master lead the way.

Today, full and part-time ministers can do the same. One of the easiest ways to develop and sustain a soul-winning culture is by sharing witnessing encounters on a weekly basis. The beauty of this approach is that these stories do not have to come from just you. In fact, it's better if they don't. Why? In two words—human nature.

Think about the last time you purchased an item at the store or online—as most do today. If it was a big-ticket item, you more than likely sought the advice of others before you decided to buy that product. If there were multiple offerings—all things such as price, features, etc. being equally the same—chances are you selected the one with the best reviews. Especially when deciding between a product with only one testimonial or an item with multiple praises.

One raving fan may win a new customer for an initial product launch. However, if you're trying to increase your sales you need more than just one testimony to thrive.

The same is true with the evangelistic culture of your church. The more your congregation hears about and sees you and others preaching the good news, the more apt they are to engage in the work themselves.

Listed below are some practical steps that you can take to embolden your church in evangelism. I can assure you, that when you implement these things in your church or ministry, you'll have a greater chance of igniting the witnessing flame within your congregants. As you consider applying these items, please note that this is not an exhaustive list.

- Purchase copies of this book and hold a 4-hour, weekend,

six-week or eight-week evangelism equipping class using this material.

- Purchase copies of this book for your ministry leaders. For additional training, you can enroll your volunteers in my online evangelism training course. The course is available at **JeffJerina.com**.

- Connect with me via email at **jeff@MenUnplugged.net** to schedule live evangelism training for your church or group.

- Tell stories of others proclaiming the gospel each week.

- Have your church members share their witnessing efforts behind the pulpit. Whenever you can, do this whether or not their actions lead to others placing their faith in Jesus.

- Create a social media page where church members can pray for one another, offer words of encouragement, and share their recent opportunities to witness.

- Whenever an individual places their faith in Jesus Christ, do your best to acknowledge that person before your assembly. Not just in the baptistery, but as soon as the new believer is comfortable with being recognized. Some of these new Christians may want others to know about their recent decision to trust Jesus as their personal Savior right away.

- Send a weekly email to the members of your congregation, encouraging them to be proactive in sharing their faith.

- Teach Bible studies about evangelism in your small groups or Sunday school classes.

> REGARDLESS OF WHETHER OR NOT THESE ACTIONS LEAD OTHERS TO CHRIST, THE FACT THAT YOUR CONGREGATION LIVES OUT THIS MINISTRY TOGETHER IS THE KEY.

Whatever your denomination is, it's never too late to encourage and equip others to testify about God's free gift of salvation. Begin with prayer. Ask the Holy Spirit for guidance and power. Equip those in your care by offering this course at your church. Lastly, remain steadfast and committed to the task of cultivating a culture of evangelism (see James 1:12; Gal. 6:9; Phil. 4:13).

In conclusion, this or any other training on evangelism will only go as far as you take it. With this in mind, please remember that sharing the gospel has to be enriched on a consistent basis. Therefore, the more you model personal evangelism for those in your church the more engaged your parishioners will become. Consequently, they'll begin to see the Great Commission as a blessing rather than a burden to fulfill. As a result, the good news of Jesus Christ will be heard within and surrounding your community. Ultimately, the lost will be found.

God speed!

Jeff

NOTES

INTRODUCTION

1 God does not want anyone to perish. Scripture states in 2 Peter 3:9, "The Lord is not slow in keeping his promise, as some understand slowness. Instead he is patient with you, not wanting anyone to perish, but everyone to come to repentance." God gave all believers the mandate to share the gospel (see Acts 1:8; Mt. 28:8-20; Mark 16:15).

2 Meyer, F.B. Expository Preaching Plans and Methods. (Eugene, OR: Wipf and Stock Publishers, 2001) 44.

3 Yohannan, K.P. Against the Wind. (Carrolton, TX: gfa books, 2004) 195.

4 Ibid., 193.

5 Coleman, Robert E. The Master Plan of Evangelism. Second edition. (Grand Rapids, MI: Revel, 2010) 89.

CHAPTER 1: PROOF IN THE NUMBERS

1 McIntosh, Gary. "What Person Led You to Faith in Christ." *The good Book Blog*, October 29, 2014, http://www.thegoodbookblog.com/2014/oct/29/what-person-led-you-to-faith-in-Christ/ (accessed August 30, 2016).

2 Ibid.

3 Strand, Brad. *Strand Study Bible*. Available at https://MenUnplugged.net/Bible. PDF, 1561.

4 Pew Research Center. "Christians remain world's largest religious group, but they are declining in Europe." April 5, 2017, http://www.pewresearch.org/fact-tank/2017/04/05/christians-remain-worlds-largest-religious-group-but-they-are-declining-in-europe/ (accessed February 12, 2019).

5 Ibid. This assertion comes from the Pew Research Center's research that there are 2.3 billion professing Christians and a total of 7.3 billion people living in the world as of 2015. Therefore, subtracting 2.3B from 7.3B is 5 billion people that would have heard the gospel in less than two and a half years.

CHAPTER 2: SOMETHING WAS MISSING

1 Other passages to cross-reference. I Sam. 13:14, "…the Lord has sought out a man after his own heart and appointed him ruler of his people…" Acts 13:22, "After removing Saul, he made David their king. God testified concerning him: 'I have found David son of Jesse, a man after my own heart; he will do everything I want him to do.'"

CHAPTER 4: SET FREE INDEED

1 Mayo Clinic. April 28, 2016, https://www.mayoclinic.org/diseases-conditions/body-dysmorphic-disorder/symptoms-causes/syc-20353938 (accessed August 30, 2019).

CHAPTER 9: HIS MISSION OUR MANDATE

1 Perspectives, Robert Coleman p 124

2 Matthew Henry Commentary on disciples being fishermen

CHAPTER 10: PRACTICE MAKES PERFECT

1 A. Scott Moreau, Gary R. Corwin, and Gary B. McGee. Introducing World Missions: A Biblical, Historical, and Practical Survey. (Grand Rapids, MI: Baker Academic, 2004) 82.

2 Piper, John. "You Shall Receive Power… for Mission." *Desiring God website*, October 16, 1988, http://www.desiringgod.org/messages/you-shall-receive-powerfor-mission (accessed July 16, 2017).

3 Slick, Matt. "The Importance of Prayer in Evangelism." CARM.org. https://carm.org/prayer-in-evangelism (accessed July 21, 2017).

CHAPTER 11: UNDERSTANDING YOUR ROLE IN EVANGELISM

[1] In my interview with top 100 Christian apologist, Sean McDowell, we spoke about practical ways believers can defend their faith. When I shared with him the importance of Christians being prepared in knowing how to share the gospel, he agreed and stated, "Because there is so much at stake." That full interview can be listened to for FREE at https://MenUnplugged.net/ep65.

2 Strand, 1938.

3 Jesus Film Project. January 5, 2017, https://www.jesusfilm.org/blog-and-stories/40-verses-about-evangelism.html (accessed July 15, 2017).

4 Wilkinson, Bruce. Prayer of Jabez. (Colorado Springs, CO: Multnomah Publishers, 2009).

CHAPTER 12: THE PROPER MOTIVE

1 Strand, 1938.

2 Jesus Christ stated His mission in Luke 19:10, which was "to seek and save those who are lost." He gave His followers (including Christians today) the mandate to do the same (see John 20:21; Mark 16:15; Mt. 18:16-20).

CHAPTER 13: OVERCOMING OBSTACLES

1 Webster's Online Dictionary. Definition for obstacle. http://www.merriam-webster.com/dictionary/obstacle (accessed September 20, 2016).

CHAPTER 14: FIVE STAGES OF WITNESSING

1 Josh McDowell and Sean McDowell. Evidence That Demands a Verdict. (Nashville, TN: Thomas Nelson, 2017) vii.

2 Ibid., vii.

CHAPTER 15: SHARING YOUR TESTIMONY

1 A. Scott Moreau, Gary R. Corwin, and Gary B. McGee. Introducing World Missions: A Biblical, Historical, and Practical Survey. (Grand Rapids, MI: Baker Academic, 2004) 62.

2 Whaley, Vernon. Called to Worship. (Nashville, TN: Thomas Nelson, 2009) 264.

3 Manning, Brennan. Abba's Child: The Cry of the Heart for Intimate Belonging. Rev. expanded ed. (Colorado Springs, CO: NavPress, 2002) 112.

ACCESS MORE RESOURCES AT
JEFFJERINA.com

ACKNOWLEDGMENTS

There are many people who have played an integral role in the creation of this book. Before mentioning these unsung heroes, I want to thank my Lord and Savior, Jesus Christ, for sparing His life for mine. Without His sacrifice, I would not be here today. At times, I have felt unworthy to write this book. In those moments and others, God's love for me removed my doubts, renewed my strength, and His Spirit guided me every step of the way. I am forever grateful for the opportunity that God has given me to complete this project.

I am grateful for my friend and trusted mentor, Brad Strand, for previewing and editing the first draft of this book. His wisdom and support have been instrumental in my walk with the Lord. Thank you for helping me understand and live out the core mission of Christendom: Reaching others for Jesus Christ.

My good friend and brother in Christ, John Christian, for which I am very grateful; his friendship and willingness to get in the foxhole with me and pray about this book and life is monumental. For always being there when I needed to vent and laugh. For being the one who gave me that extra motivation and courage to press on.

My sincere gratitude for every Men Unplugged listener. Their feedback and support motivate me to keep interviewing, speaking, and creating resources (like this book) to help Christians ignite their faith in Jesus, and succeed in every aspect of life.

Thank you to Madison Weatherbee for helping me with the cover design. As a visionary, I am always amazed when I see how quickly and easily artists like Madison can catch the vision for a work and then make that idea come to fruition on paper.

I am thankful for each person who has endorsed this book. They are truly mammoths of the faith. To have them take the time to read and endorse this work is humbling, inspiring, and an honor to say the least. Special thanks to Josh McDowell, for writing the Foreword to this book.

My heartfelt thanks to my mom and dad, for always pushing me to be my best. They never gave up on me—even during those dark years of my life—when I was far from God, with no hope in sight.

Two of my greatest blessings are my two children. My daughter, Kinley, and son, Eli, who continually inspire me with their boundless energy, fearless nature, and zest for life.

And as always, I want to thank my wife, Amy, for the endless support, love, and grace that she has shown me throughout our marriage. From the very beginning (when all I had was the idea to write this book) to the last word I penned, she has sacrificed her time and energy so I could finish this task. As the catalyst behind this book, she has been there every step of the way, praying with me, praying for me (more than I will ever know), and encouraging me to write this book.

ABOUT THE AUTHOR

J eff Jerina is the founder and host of Men Unplugged (a Christ-centered talk show and resource for men and their families) and a graduate of Liberty Theological Seminary. On the *Men Unplugged podcast*, Jeff and well-known Christian leaders provide listeners around the world with practical tips and solutions to succeed in every aspect of life. For more than 18 years, he has been speaking and teaching on a variety of topics, including: Evangelism, leadership, personal development, and men's issues.

He is a frequent guest on national radio shows and podcasts. Jeff is the founder and CEO of SiteSpartan.com, a website design, hosting, and digital marketing company.

As a Christian pastor and public speaker, he loves to interact with and entertain audiences in ways that create lasting impact. Jeff has been known to juggle, perform card tricks, and do the moonwalk on stage. He enjoys teaching others through his keynote speeches, courses, and group training forums.

He spends most of his time now speaking, writing, developing courses, and managing Men Unplugged.

He and his wife, Amy, live in Texas with their two children.

www.JeffJerina.com

ABOUT MEN UNPLUGGED

Dubbed "A MUST FOR EVERY MAN", Men Unplugged helps men **ignite** their faith, **strengthen** their family, and **succeed** in life.

www.MenUnplugged.net

CONTACT JEFF

To get the latest *Faith Without Fear* updates and resources, visit:

- **JeffJerina.com/Books/FaithWithoutFear**

Jeff speaks frequently on a variety of topics and is a featured guest on podcasts and radio programs. He can deliver a keynote, emcee, conference, or seminar content depending on your needs. If you are interested in finding out more, please visit his speaking page at:

- **JeffJerina.com/Speaking**

To get the latest updates about *Men Unplugged,* a Christ-centered talk show and resource for men (of any age and stage of life) and their families, please visit:

- **MenUnplugged.net**

You can also connect with Jeff here:

- Personal email: jeff@MenUnplugged.net
- Contact Page: **JeffJerina.com/Contact**

Other books, courses, and training:

- **JeffJerina.com**

Mind Over Muscle
The Rocket Fuel to the
Faith Without Fear
method for sharing your
faith

Jeff Jerina

Available in audio and print
formats.

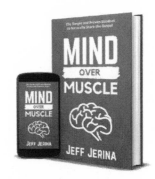

Say Goodbye to Lost Opportunities and Difficult Conversations with Non-Believers

Mind Over Muscle is the turbo boost to:

- Changing your spiritual mindset.
- Sharing the gospel.
- Maintaining the eternal perspective.
- Crushing your daily fears.

It's 28 minutes of additional audio to help you go the next level in your own witnessing efforts. *Mind Over Muscle* is the simple and proven mindset that helps Christians share their faith to anyone at any time. It's the rocket fuel to the *Faith Without Fear* method for sharing your faith. PDF included with audio file.

Available online at:
https://JeffJerina.com/Mind-Over-Muscle

Faith Without Fear
How to Share What You
Believe with Confidence
and Power

Jeff Jerina

Available in paperback, e-book, and audio formats.

Also Available in Online Course, Live and Virtual Training Formats.

To learn more visit JeffJerina.com/Training or
connect with Jeff at JeffJerina.com/Contact

No matter your age, vocation, or biblical knowledge, you'll be encouraged and equipped to easily share your faith to anyone at any time. This training will:

- Teach you a simple, natural method for sharing the gospel.
- Help you understand your role in evangelism.
- Equip you with the ULTIMATE tool for sharing your faith.
- Remove any fear you have about witnessing.
- Remind you that your personal story of salvation matters.

Available online at:
https://JeffJerina.com/Books/FaithWithoutFear

For bulk discounts, visit:
https://JeffJerina.com/Contact

To Register for the Online Course, visit:
https://JeffJerina.com/Courses

Power and Purpose
A Practical Guide for
Living Your True Purpose

Jeff Jerina

Available for FREE.

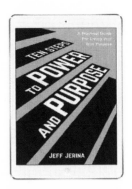

Discover The Proven Principles That Will
Help You Live Your God-Given Design!

Power and Purpose is the proven path to discover and live your true purpose.

As a FREE resource, you'll learn:

- What motivates and drives you.
- Your spiritual gifts.
- How to maximize your innate abilities.
- How to overcome obstacles that are holding you back.
- And more…

You will have the opportunity to chat with Jeff about additional coaching regarding your purpose and calling.

Available online at:
https://JeffJerina.com/Free-Book

For personal or group training on this material, including an additional module titled *Clarify Your Calling*, please email Jeff@MenUnplugged.net.

MEN UNPLUGGED PODCAST

Weekly interviews, biblical wisdom, and actionable steps to help you strengthen your faith and succeed in life.

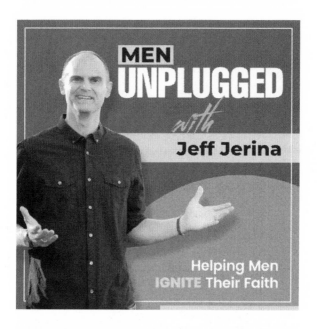

On the weekly talk show, Jeff Jerina and well-known Christian leaders discuss key topics to help you go the next level in your faith, family, health, finances, career, discipleship, and more. Listened to by hundreds of thousands across the globe, *Men Unplugged* has been dubbed by many as "A Must for Every Man."

Available online and podcast platforms, including: Apple, Google, and Spotify.

Subscribe and Listen for FREE at:
MenUnplugged.net/Podcast

MEN UNPLUGGED COMMUNITY

Helping Christian men EXCEL
as MEN of GOD!

In this private Community of Men Unplugged, we help men take the guesswork out of biblical manhood so they can experience God's best for their life.

In addition to Powerful Transformation, each man will be encouraged and equipped with Christ-Centered Fellowship, Brotherhood, Support, Biblical Wisdom, Bonus Interviews, and more.

Join the Community Today at:
MenUnplugged.net/Community

COACHING and SPEAKING

(JJ) JEFF JERINA

Jeff speaks frequently on the topic of spiritual rest and renewal. He can deliver a keynote, half-day, or full-day version of this content, depending on your needs.

In addition to this training, Jeff speaks on a variety of topics, including: His testimony; personal development; leadership; evangelism; discipleship; a biblical response to today's global events; faith-driven entrepreneurship; and men's ministry.

If you have another topic that you think Jeff would be a great fit for, please let him know. He would love to hear your thoughts.

To book Jeff for a speaking event, please visit his Speaking page at:

- JeffJerina.com/Speaking

For personal coaching, please visit his Training page at:

- JeffJerina.com/Training

URGENT PLEA!

Thank You for Reading My Book!

I really appreciate all your feedback,
and I love hearing what you have to say.

I need your input to make the next version of this book,
online training, as well as future books better.

Please leave me a helpful review on Amazon letting me
know what you thought of *Faith Without Fear*.

You can do that through this link:
https://JeffJerina.com/ReviewFWF

Thanks so much!

~ Jeff Jerina

Made in the USA
Columbia, SC
10 September 2022

66946784R00119